MITCHELL BE

TOURING IN WINE COUNTRY

TUSCANY

MAUREEN ASHLEY MW

SERIES EDITOR

HUGH JOHNSON

Contents

Dedication
For Gloria, whose extraordinary kindness and care brought bright rays of light into an otherwise dark time.

Touring in Wine Country
Tuscany
edited and designed by
Mitchell Beazley
part of Reed Consumer Books Limited
Michelin House, 81 Fulham Road
London SW3 6RB

First published in 1996

Reprinted 1996, 1998

A CIP catalogue record of this book is available from the British Library

ISBN 1 85732 582 6

Editors: Susan Keevil, Lucy Bridgers, Diane Pengelly
Art Editor: Paul Drayson
Index: Angie Hipkin
Gazetteer: Sally Chorley
Production: Juliette Butler
Managing Editor: Sue Jamieson
Executive Art Editor: Susan Downing
Art Director: Gaye Allen
Cartography: Map Creation Limited
Design by the Bridgewater Book Company
Illustrations: Polly Raines

Typeset in Bembo and Gill Sans

Printed and bound by Toppan Printing Company, China

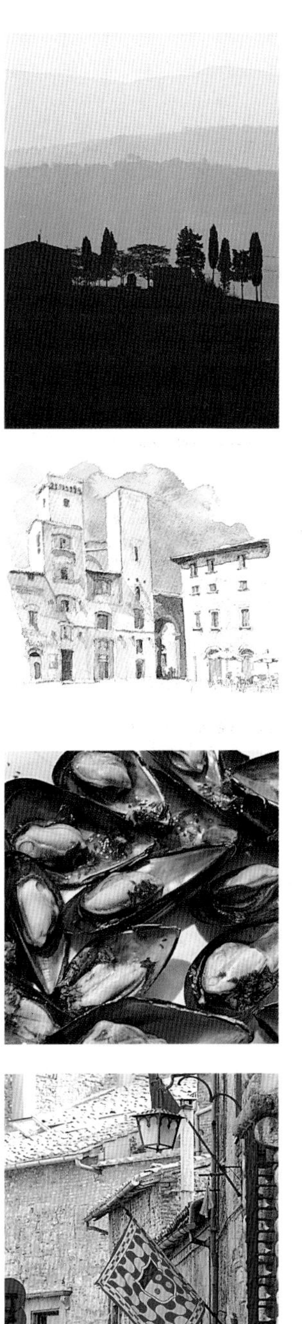
MOSAICO

Foreword

Why is it that wine tasted in the cellar (or even in the region) of its birth has a magic, a vibrancy and vigour that makes it so memorable?

It is easy to think of physical reasons. The long journey to the supermarket shelf cannot be without some effect on a living creature - and wine is indeed alive, and correspondingly fragile.

It is even easier to think of romantic reasons: the power of association, the atmosphere and scents of the cellar, the enthusiasm of the grower as he moves from barrel to barrel....

No wonder wine touring is the first-choice holiday for so many people. It is incomparably the best way to understand wine - whether at the simple level of its scenery and culture, or deeper into the subtleties of its terroirs and the different philosophies of different producers.

There are armchair wine-books, coffee-table books, quick reference wine-books...even a pop-up wine book. Now with this series we have the wine-traveller's precise, pin-pointed practical guide to sleuthing through the regions that have most to offer, finding favourites and building up memories. The bottles you find yourself have the genie of experience in them.

Hugh Johnson

Tuscany

Those who experience sensory overload from the surfeit of artistic wonders in Florence are said to be suffering from Stendhal's syndrome. There is no recognized equivalent for those overwhelmed by Tuscany's natural beauties – but there should be. It is impossible to travel through the region and remain unmoved by its grace, its wildness, its shapes, colours and panoramas. Its variety is enthralling: bare crests give way to pine forests, wheat fields, olive groves and villas, and row after row of neatly tended vines – all punctuated by inspiring villas. Combined with good wine, good food and the Tuscans themselves, it is more than enough to engender a life-time's love-affair.

Tuscany is joyous at any time of year. Spring is wonderful, with almond and cherry blossom, lush green wheat and sprouting vines. In summer, cool hill slopes, fresh coastal breezes and plentiful shade prevent overheating, although August, when most Italians (including city restaurateurs) are on holiday, can be a bit frenetic. Autumn brings renewed tranquillity and the heady aromas of the harvest. Even winter brings compensations: roads are clear; bare vines reveal their carefully pruned forms; mimosa brings a splash of colour and bright, crisp days give incomparable views.

Much of the landscape has been shaped by the region's countless wars and by the *mezzadria*, the old crop-sharing system. Fortified towns and villages were built high with castles on the more commanding positions as a result of continuous battles between rival dukedoms, principalities and city states. The *mezzadria* landowners lived in large, imposing villas surrounded by stables, granaries, wine cellars, oil presses, a chapel and more while the share croppers' small *case coloniche* (farmhouses) dotted their land. As the system broke down, some estates consolidated, bought back land

Left *Travelling through Tuscany raises the spirits and calms the soul whatever the weather.*

Top *A characteristic painted doorway in Montecatini, province of Pistoia.*

from their ex-*mezzadri,* (who moved on to more lucrative jobs in the cities) and concentrated on one or two crops rather than the old polyculture. Others fragmented as the peasant farmers bought land, and formed the network of small quality-conscious growers, who have done so much to raise Tuscany's image.

THE ENOTECA

Most towns and many villages sport at least one *enoteca*, or wine shop. Some concentrate on local wines, others stock the more important Tuscan/Italian wines too. Occasionally they can be tasted. Some *enoteche* serve snacks, others place a greater emphasis on food and are more like wine bars.

TRAVELLING AROUND

It is easier to find your way around some provinces than others. There are nine in all, each responsible for its local road signs. Some are more effective than others – in Pisa, for example, you may feel like resorting to a compass. There is a good network of *autostrade* (motorways) and *superstrade* (toll-free dual-carriageways). Not all are on maps, so follow signs (blue for *autostrade,* green otherwise). If planning to use the *autostrada* system a lot, consider buying a Viacard, a debit card for the tolls. Otherwise avoid this, and residents' credit system lanes, unless you enjoy making Italians irate.

Most town centres are now pedestrianized with well sign-posted car parks around them. Some are pay-and-display, but many of the machines are not yet converted to accept new coinage introduced in 1995, so hang on to any old coins.

The local tourist office will supply much information, but if you cannot find it, try looking for Azienda Provinciale Turismo (APT) in the Yellow Pages under Enti Turistiche.

Note: It is quite common for the electricity to be cut during storms and street lighting can fail. So take a torch.

Above *The rolling hills around San Gimignano, where Vernaccia is made into full, dry white wine.*

Central Italy

— - — - —	Regione boundary
Zagarolo	White wine
Chianti	Red wine
TORGIANO	Red and white wine
VIN SANTO	Dessert wine
[Sassicaia]	Selected Vino da Tavola

DOC boundaries are distinguished by coloured lines

[115]	Area mapped at larger scale on page shown
▭	Land above 600 metres

1:1,500,000

Km. 0 20 40 Km.
Miles 0 10 20 30 Miles

COLLI BOLOGNESI
EMILIA-ROMAGNA
Colline Lucchesi
Bianco della Valdinievole
Lucca
Montecatini Terme
Pistoia
Bianco dell' Empolese
Carmignano
Prato
Imola
Lugo
Albana di Romagna
Faenza
Ravenna
Sangiovese di Romagna
Cagnina di Romagna
Rosso Armentano
Forlì
Trebbiano di Romagna
Borgo San Lorenzo
Cervia
Barbarossa
Chianti
Firenze
Rufina
Pagadebit di Romagna
Cesena
Cesenatico
POMINO
Santa Cristina
Tignanello
VIN SANTO
Vernaccia di San Gimignano
Colli Fiorentini
Figline
Poggibonsi
Colli Senesi
Chianti Classico
Rimini
SAN MARINO
Galestro
Sangiovese di Romagna
Cattolica
Siena
Montevarchi
Chianti
Chianti
Arezzo
Sansepolcro
Pesaro
Sangiovese dei Colli Pesaresi
Fano
Val d'Arbia
Urbino
Falerio dei Colli Ascolani
Bianchello del Metauro
Metauro
Rosso di Montalcino
Cortona
Bianco Vergine Valdichiana
Città di Castello
COLLI ALTOTIBERINI
Moscadello di Montalcino
Senigallia
Montepulciano
Vino Nobile di Montepulciano
Umbertide
Lacrima di Morro
COLLI DEL TRASIMENO
Gubbio
Verdicchio dei Castelli di Jesi
Rosso Piceno
Iesi
Ancona
Lago di Trasimeno
Perugia
Fabriano
Esino
Verdicchio di Matelica
MARCHE
Rosso Conero
COLLI PERUGINI
TORGIANO
ASSISI
Assisi
Orvieto
UMBRIA
di Pitigliano
Rosso d'Arquata
Rosso Piceno
Aleatico di Gradoli
Orvieto
Orvieto Classico
Foligno
Montefalco
Vernaccia di Serrapetrona
Macerata
Lago di Bolsena
Bianco dei Colli Maceratesi
Chienti
Montefiascone
COLLI MARTANI
Orvieto
Tuscania
Spoleto
Nera
Fermo
Viterbo
COLLI AMERINI
Norcia
Terni
Narni
Caprarola
Ascoli Piceno
Fontanelle
Rosso Piceno Superiore
Tronto
Civita Castellana
Rieti
Lago di Bracciano
Bracciano
Bianco Capena
Teramo
LAZIO
Montepulciano d'Abruzzo
L'Aquila
ROMA
Tivoli
Trebbiano
Fiorano
Frascati
MACCARESE
Marino
Zagarolo
Cesanese di Olevano Romano
Cerasuolo d'Abruzzo
Pescara
Tevere
Turano
Reno
Santerno
Fiora
Arbia
31, 42
82

Above *Entrance to the Parrina estate in southwest Tuscany. Visiting Tuscany's wines estates not only unveils the secrets of the wines, but gives a closer understanding of the region as a whole.*

Visiting estates

Most Italians are wonderfully hospitable and (winemakers especially) love to talk about their work, so it is seldom difficult to arrange to visit an estate. For most producers, however, making wine is their livelihood, not a hobby or a sideline, and they simply cannot drop everything for an hour or so whenever a passer-by expresses an interest. So it is imperative to telephone first for an appointment. A day or two before is usually enough; more than a couple of weeks may be too long.

It can be hard to arrange a visit around the first weekend of April, as most producers will be at Italy's important wine fair in Verona. January and August are the most common holiday periods. Harvest – late August to mid-October – is an exciting experience, but producers are even more hard-pressed than usual and may have little time for visitors.

Estates vary widely in what they offer. Some give a full tour of vineyards, winemaking and ageing cellars, followed by a tasting. Others may show a video or offer only a tasting. Usually tastings are free. You are not expected to buy anything but it may be courteous to do so. Some estates offer refreshments, even meals. Others produce and sell complementary products such as olive oil and honey.

AGRITURISMO

Many estates have set up *agriturismo*, or 'green tourism' ventures, which began as a way of giving townsfolk an insight into country life, but developed into a pleasant, inexpensive way of staying in the Italian countryside. Furnished apartments or rooms in villas on a wine, olive or general farming estate are rented out for a minimum of one week. *Agriturismo* is incredibly popular, however, and apartments need booking well in advance. Standards vary widely too: some are delightful traditional Tuscan farmhouses, well-appointed with swimming pools, others are depressing, so it best to book through a reliable agency.

Viticulture, vinification and wine law

As far as is known, Tusany has been producing wine since Etruscan times. Nevertheless, it is only in the past decade that the majority of wines have become so exciting. Much of the development has been led by consultants, dedicated men and women with rare skills in extracting the best from each plot of land.

GROWING GRAPES

Whether stretching over tens of hectares or dotted in tiny plots, most Tuscan vineyards are neatly planted on a tidy grid, stretched carefully along wires. Most new plantings now have 4,000 or more vines per hectare, almost twice the previous density. Despite the costs and vastly increased labour, growers have taken the plunge as quality benefits. They have also been careful to replant better-quality clones.

Vines are usually trained low so that they gain reflected warmth from the ground and waste less energy supporting unproductive woody growth. The main training systems are cordon spur, where the trunk of the vine is trained in an inverted L-shape and each season's growth starts from a series of spurs left on the horizontal; and guyot, where the trunk is a stump from which one or two canes from one year's fruiting shoots are trained horizontally to provide those for the next year. Pruning during the vines' winter rest period reforms these shapes and, vitally, restricts growth. Wine laws specify a maximum yield but the best growers aim even lower, sometimes lopping burgeoning bunches to concentrate the quality of the remaining grapes.

The vine's growth starts in early spring, when buds are susceptible to frost damage. A patch of warm weather will see shoots spurt remarkably quickly and keep growers busy attaching the new growth to wires. The vine flowers between late spring and early summer. Fine weather is crucial to ensure a full pollination and avoid malformed or partially formed berries – an annual concern.

During the growing season some growers leave the grasses that spring up around the vines to fix the topsoil, others plough them in for humus, a few treat them with herbicides. As the grape bunches form, growers often trim foliage to improve the grapes' exposure to light and sun. Grapes develop their colour in the month before full ripeness. A little rain is welcome at this point to flesh them out, especially if the summer has been hot and dry.

The harvest itself (which starts in late August for some white varieties and continues into October for reds) needs dry conditions. Wet weather leads to dilution, rot – and profoundly depressed producers.

Far left *Picking is still best done by hand to ensure the healthiest grapes are chosen.*
Left *Traditionally Tuscan reds have been aged in large oak casks called* botti. *Recently there has been a trend towards smaller, new oak French* barriques *and producers have been experimenting with woods of different sources and ages.*
Below *Most Tuscan estates have invested in hygienic, stainless steel vats with good temperature control.*

GRAPE VARIETIES

Most Tuscan reds are based on Sangiovese, an excellent variety which can turn out reasonable wine quite easily but is difficult to master. Blending in small quantities of other grapes (often Canaiolo, Mammolo or Ciliegiolo) for extra complexity is common practice. Traditional white grapes are Trebbiano and Malvasia, which need skillful winemaking to give fine wine.

Recent years have seen many experiments in Tuscany with non-traditional varieties, particularly red Cabernet Sauvignon, Merlot and Syrah and the whites Chardonnay and Sauvignon.

Above *Vernaccia di San Gimignano, which can produce full-bodied, dry wines.*

MAKING THE WINE

The colour, flavour and tannin in red wine comes from the grape skins, so grapes for red wine are first of all crushed, to bring the skins and juice into contact. The skins remain with the juice during fermentation. The winemaker decides the best temperature at which to ferment and how long to leave the juice on the skins. Most Tuscan reds then go into large wooden casks to 'soften' or add a little vanilla-like silkiness. The casks, or *botti,* are usually made from Slovenian oak and are sometimes a century or more old. More recently there has been a trend to use small, new French-oak *barriques.*

The fresh fruitiness of white wines comes from pressing the grapes immediately after picking to separate juice from the skins. The juice is then fermented on its own. Tuscan whites are most often aged in stainless steel; only a few are put into oak. Italians love drinking white wine very young

Below *Sangiovese is often blended with small quantities of other varieties but also makes an excellent wine on its own.*

Malvasia (top) *and Trebbiano* (centre), *once used in Chianti, are now more commonly made into crisp, dry wine.*

and even the top growers find it hard to resist their customers' demand and sell them ever earlier in the season.

Sweet Vin Santo, or 'Holy wine', is made all over Tuscany from dried raisin-like grapes, whose juice is fermented very slowly in tiny *caratelli* (barrels) containing *madre*, debris from the previous years' wine. The *caratelli* are sealed and left for three years or more before the wine is released and bottled.

WINE CLASSIFICATION

Italy's first wine rules were designed in the early 1960s, with the categories *Vino da Tavola* (VdT, simple 'table wine'), *Denominazione di Origine Controllata* (DOC, 'quality' wines) and DOCG (the 'G' for *e Garantita*, supposedly a super-category starting up in the early 1980s). At this time the Italian wine scene was at its worst: poor practices were rife, and the aim quantity, not quality.

As producers became increasingly experimental and innovative and quality became the industry's ethos, many found DOC(G) constraints a hindrance. Frequently they ignored them, making the best wines they could regardless. Officialy just VdT wine, each was given a *nome di fantasia*, prominent on the label. This widespread practice and a few bureaucratic misjudgements brought the wine law into such disrepute that a complete revision was called for. It was published in 1992 and is gradually coming into effect.

Only the most basic wines will now be VdT. A new category, Indicazione Geografica Tipica (IGT) covers broadly regional wine styles, while new, stricter DOC(G)s will be created for sub-zones even as small as individual vineyards. Thus classifications will be nested like a Russian doll and, in any year, wine not up to the standard of the area's tightest DOC(G) may be declassified one or more levels.

Food and eating out

Top *Onions, grown widely, are important for flavouring as is garlic.* Above *Fresh* cozze *mussels are plentiful along the coast as are many varieties of fish and seafood.*

Throughout Tuscany food is wholesome and fairly simple. Olive oil is used liberally and the diet strongly meat-oriented. Bread is firm and unsalted, except for rich, flat *scacciata*. The only variation is along the coast where freshly caught fish naturally predominates, especially in summer.

EATING OUT

You are unlikely to eat badly in Tuscany. Pop into any *trattoria* (avoiding any aimed specifically at tourists, with menus in several languages or spattered with odd English phrases) and the meal will normally be enjoyable. If, as you look in, you see the oil in the cruet is a beautiful deep green colour, you can look forward to the meal with even more confidence.

It is more difficult, however, to be confident about the wine. Even in the heart of a wine zone there may be no more on offer than a carafe of house wine; it might be divine or it might be dreary. If in doubt, the red is a safer bet.

The only other possible difficulty may be the lack of a written menu. Even in good restaurants it may simply be recited to you at break-neck speed. Just gesticulate for a slower repetition or if the waiter or owner offers to choose for you, let him. He will be delighted. In any event, eating out is generally far less formal than in the UK. There is no dress code either. And children are expected to join in the feast.

Restaurants and *trattorie* close one or one-and-a-half days a week, especially in towns, and there is little consensus as to when. It is always worth booking first.

Above *Florence's bustling San Lorenzo market.*
Bottom Pappardelle, *flat, broad noodles, are one of the most typical pasta shapes in Tuscany.*

THE TUSCAN MEAL

A meal typically begins with antipasti of *crostini*, small rounds of bread covered with minced chicken liver, *milza* (spleen) or other topping; or *bruschetta*, toasted Tuscan bread rubbed with garlic, drenched in olive oil and possibly topped with tomatoes or black cabbage. There is usually also a plate of *salumi* – salami and cured meats.

The first course, the *primo*, is often pasta, usually *pappardelle*, flat, broad strips; *pinci* or *pici*, thick, hand-rolled spaghetti (a speciality of Montepulciano and Montalcino) or ravioli, filled with meat or spinach and ricotta. Sauces are commonly meat based; *lepre* (hare), *coniglio* (rabbit) and *anatra* (duck) are the classics with *funghi* (mushroom) sauces and *tartufi* (truffles) are popular in season. Alternatively, there are thick soups that rank as *cucina povera*, 'poor folk's food'. *Ribollita* is a slow-cooked vegetable mass with bread for bulk and thickening; *zuppa di pane* is literally bread soup but given a lift, usually by tomatoes; *panzanella* is a cold summer version, more like salad than soup. More substantial are pulse-based soups; various combinations of *fagioli* (white kidney beans), *lenticchie* (lentils), *ceci* (chick peas) and *farro* (a barley-like grain) dominate.

On to the *secondo*, the main course. The flagship is *La Fiorentina*, a giant grilled T-bone steak from the local *Chianina* cattle (or *Maremmana* cattle in the south). *Agnello* (lamb) and *pollo* (chicken) are popular, as are *coniglio*, *lepre*, or *salsiccia* (meaty sausage). Many places will serve three or four 'taster' portions together. A great speciality is *trippa* (tripe), usually cooked with tomatoes. *Fagioli* are also commonly used as an alternative to seasonal vegetables or an (often unexciting) salad.

Tuscans are rightfully proud of their cheeses. *Pecorino*, from ewe's milk, can either be *fresco* (young and soft) or *stagionato* (matured, hard and stronger). *Caprino* is goat's milk cheese.

For *dolce* or dessert, most typical are *cantucci* (almond biscuits), best dunked in a glass of Vin Santo. Other desserts are often bought-in. Traditional Tuscan desserts are less rich than these: cake-like and dryish, often made with chestnut flour – always worth indulging in if *fatti a casa* (home-made).

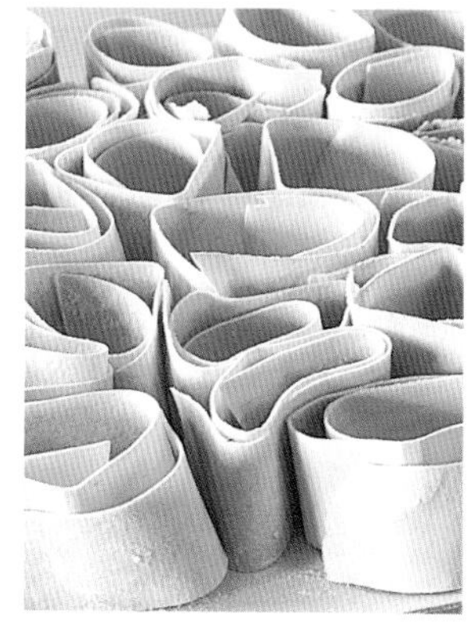

FOOD SHOPPING

Italians still prefer to shop daily at small specialist shops, so few supermarkets offer the range and quality of the UK chains. However every town has its butcher, cheese shop and *salumeria* (for cured meats, salami, prosciutto etc) and fresh bread is widely available, as are fruit and vegetables. Most towns also have daily (morning) markets. Just remember that shops close in the early afternoon while shopkeepers are eating or sleeping.

Olive oil

Although Tuscany is usually regarded primarily as a wine region and its olive oil as merely a complementary crop, the abundance of olive trees and the spasmodic nature of vineyards (except in Chianti Classico, Montepulciano and Montalcino) suggest that it should be the reverse. Olive oil is as central to Tuscany's agricultural economy as it is to its diet.

The glories of Tuscan extra virgin olive oil swiftly came to notice in 1985. In January of that year, a cold snap of rare force hit Italy. Temperatures were so low that many olive trees were killed off and most were reduced to bare stumps, changing the scenery drastically and, naturally, the price of oil soared. The resultant publicity stimulated northern Europe's fascination with fine olive oil. Now healthy new growth has sprouted from thick, old trunks and many producers have taken the opportunity of replacing old trees with newer, better varieties and plantation systems. The interest in fine oil remains undiminished and demand keeps prices for the best extra virgin buoyant.

Making fine olive oil is expensive and labour-intensive. There is as much debate concerning the best varieties,

Below *Olive oil, flavoured with bay, chilli and fennel. It is best, though, enjoyed 'straight' for its fruity, sometimes spicy, tones.*

pruning systems and plantation densities as there is for vines. Generally olive trees need much more separation – as much as ten metres. Olives should be stripped by hand. Nets may be hung underneath to catch them, but not too low as the olives will be bruised as they land. Bruising increases acidity, thus reducing the oil's quality: once acidity exceeds one percent, the oil can no longer be 'extra' and becomes simply 'virgin'. Most good oil has barely a third of this proportion of acid.

Top *Olive trees are never far from sight in Tuscany and in some areas, such as around Lucca, the Central Hills and the Maremma, they dominate the landscape.*
Above *Top-quality olive oil can lift even the most mundane dishes, such as these* bruschette.

The olive harvest can stretch over several months, starting just after the grape harvest. The earlier-picked olives are still green, the later-picked ones more purple, and the taste of the oil changes from zippy and peppery, to sweeter and more fruity.

In a traditional *frantoio* (oil processing plant) the olives are washed and put in an open granite grinder where they are slowly crushed. The pulp is spread on round mats called *fiscoli* which are then slipped onto the press. Pressure is applied and the olive liquid is separated from the solids. At this point the liquid is a mixture of oil and water. Most producers use a centrifuge to separate them but a few prefer to leave the liquid to settle and skim off the oil as it rises. The best oil is then ready, unfiltered, but many producers lightly filter the oil for extra clarity.

Large estates may have their own *frantoio* but most growers take their olives to one located nearby. Some have mechanised the process and are convinced that quality does not suffer. There are initiatives to regulate Tuscan oil: special regulations already exist for oils from Chianti Classico.

Above *Some vineyards, such as this one in Chianti Classico, are signposted. Many are not, but this guide tells you exactly what lies where.*

How to use this guide

Anyone touring Tuscany equipped simply with a map, could not help but find vineyards along the way, plus olive groves, charming medieval villages and perhaps the odd wine estate shop. The route would be beautiful – in Tuscany, you can hardly fail to find terrific scenery, and you would come home inspired. But you would not, unless you were very lucky, see the finest tracts of vineyard; understand why vines grow where they do; know if the wine you bought was as good as the district could produce, or was typical or unusual. The aim of this book is to help you achieve these aims. It is for anyone who, at least sometime during their trip, would like to see the vines and wine estates, taste the wines, meet producers and learn a little about their craft without ignoring Tuscany's other important splendours.

The book takes the form of a series of shortish routes, trips which could take anything between half an hour and

the best part of a day. Each route takes you through a particular part of Tuscany's wine lands. If wine is an adjunct to a more general tour, pick any route coinciding with wherever you are. Alternatively, let one route lead to the next.

The most convenient stopping-off places are pointed out too, together with recommendations for one or two places to stay. The guide itself begins and ends in Florence, but the tour can be joined at any point. Those driving up from Rome could start at Grosseto (p99), those flying to Pisa could start there (p122). Those heading along the Autostrada del Sole could pick up the route at Arezzo (p78). You can skip bits along the way or plunge in even deeper: the itineraries take all needs into account. The approximate timings given are based on the assumption that within wine areas you will move at a fairly leisurely pace, stopping from time to time; while between the wine areas you will drive reasonably fast.

WINE PRODUCERS

Thumb-nail sketches of local producers form an important part of the book. Those that are included have been chosen mainly for the quality of their wines but also for their location along the routes. So, if an estate is not included it does not necessarily mean its wines are not up to scratch, it could simply be that it is situated too far off the beaten track.

MAPS

Wine maps (see below) illustrating main routes are included.

RESTAURANTS

There are suggestions for eating out, from the smartest restaurant to the simplest *trattoria,* many with tables outdoors in summer and most featuring good wines, be they the more esoteric bottles or simply unusually good house wine. The better shops are listed too, for those self-catering, planning picnics, or wanting something intriguing to take home, and naturally the *enoteche,* places to buy and taste wine are highlighted.

HOTELS

For winelovers, *agriturismo* apartments are often the best place to stay when in Tuscany (see p13). Hotels have been suggested where there is special wine interest, or other attractions.

PLACES OF INTEREST

Tuscany is steeped in history and cultural interest and details of the most interesting places are included, as well as any special events with a wine or food interest.

Florence

For a city with one of the world's most important wine districts on its doorstep, Florence is reticent about its wine links. There is not an *enotecha* on every corner, nor are there shops full of wine memorabilia. Perhaps Florence has so many other attractions it can afford to ignore those outside its gates. Admittedly, wine is not ignored completely, but if you want to spend a few days among the splendours of this city without thinking about wine too much, it can easily be done.

And what splendours they are. The alluring *Duomo* (cathedral), visible for miles around but surprisingly squat when you are beside it, is the focal point. The Palazzo Vecchio, almost like a cardboard cut-out, overlooks the elegant Piazza della Signoria, which is a good spot to watch the world go by over an (expensive) drink, as is the more bustling Piazza della Repubblica. The Ponte Vecchio, lined with jewellery shops, and its pavements crowded with street traders, is the Arno's most atmospheric bridge, but others (and there are several) give better views of the city and of the river itself. Depending on the time of year, the Arno can be a languorous trickle or a surging torrent. There is also the Franciscan church of Santa Croce and its severe, rectangular piazza; the Medici Palace and the church of San Lorenzo; the church of Santa Maria Novella near the station and the convent of San Marco, which is now a museum.

Queues for the Uffizi gallery are often long but no wonder, considering its unrivalled collection of Renaissance art. The Pitti Palace houses a further impressive collection, and a museum. For relief, the Boboli Gardens are beautifully designed and offer cool strolls and splendid views. Even better views are seen from Piazzale Michelangelo, just outside the city walls. The walls themselves are captivating, still

The ubiquitous olive tree (top) *is as much a powerful symbol of rural Tuscany as the magnificent Renaissance Duomo* (left) *which dominates the Florence skyline, is of its capital city.*

SAL MCCCCLXX

standing in spite of the incessant traffic, as is the huge old fortress, Fortezza da Basso.

And so on and so on until your feet are sore and your head is overwhelmed – and you still will have done little more than brush the surface of this stunning city.

The quieter narrow, cobbled streets of Florence are relaxing to stroll through, and reveal a city where aesthetic appeal is found worked into delightful detail on roofs, cornices and even lamp posts. Alternatively, try the smart shopping streets in and around the Via dei Calzaiuoli and Via Tornabuoni. They are wonderful for window-shopping – unless your credit card feels strong enough for a purchase.

Eventually, however, you will need to sit down and feed the body as well as the soul and it is at this point that your thoughts may return to wine.

Above *Fresh fruit and vegetables at the main San Lorenzo market.* Left *Santa Maria Novella's splendid façade.*

WINE IN FLORENCE

Most restaurants and *trattorie* will have a decent selection of Chianti Classico and other local wines so drinking well with meals is not a problem. *Vinerie* (singular: *vineria*) are the city's old wine bars. A *vineria* is not chic, being more the haunt of elderly men swigging down small glasses filled to the rim, but they are fun and bursting with character. There is one by the central San Lorenzo market and more famous *vinerie* in Piazza del l'Olio, Via dei Cimatori, Via dei Neri and the San Pierino arch.

If you want to buy wine, move away from the central touristy areas towards the areas where Florentines live, around the Via de' Serragli in Oltrarno (the southern side of the Arno), for example, which boasts a wine equipment shop, or north of Piazza San Marco. Traditional wine shops are called *Fiaschetterie*, after the flasks (*fiaschi*) in which Chianti was once sold. Some look rather down-at-heel but may be Aladdin's caves inside. There are also a number of smarter, more modern wine shops springing up, usually called *Enoteche* (see p10), although at least one, in Via de'Serragli, calls itself a *Bottiglioteca*. Clearly Florentines, in naming as well as everything else, are very style-conscious.

Florence also has several excellent book shops with a range of books (in Italian) on all aspects of wine.

While wandering around Oltrarno you may come across a grand building called Palazzo del Vino. This was intended

RESTAURANTS

Enoteca Pinchiorri
Via Ghibellina *Tel: 055 242777*
Super-smart, super-expensive: one of Italy's best known. Astounding wine list. Menu *degustazione vinicoli* is a tasting menu with a different wine for each course. Prices are staggering.

Cantinetta Antinori
Piazza Antinori *Tel: 055 292234*
Full range of Antinori wines. Incongruously, wine bar layout but elegant and formal menu, food and service. Tuscan specialities are offered.

Ristorante alle Murate
Via Ghibellina *Tel: 055 240618*
Relaxed Tuscan elegance. Short, traditional, delicious menu. Extensive wine selection. Mid-priced.

Don Chisciotte
Via C Ridolfi *Tel: 055 475430*
Smart, elegant; good choice of well put-together dishes. Well chosen wines.

Above *The central San Lorenzo market has plentiful supplies of* salumi *and cheeses.*

Pepolino
Borgo Ognissanti *Tel: 055 287515*
Quiet, refined. Intriguing food. Good wine list.

Le Mosacce
Via Proconsolo *Tel: 055 294361*
Fast-moving *trattoria*. House wine decent, Chianti good.

Pane e Vino
Via San Niccolò *Tel: 055 2476956*
Ex-*enoteca*. Hundreds of wines; formal tastings. Good cheeses. Mid-priced.

Cibreo (1)
Via dei Macci *Tel: 055 2341100*
Welcoming and well known. Classic dishes. Good wine choice.

Cibreo (2)
Piazza Ghiberti *Tel: 055 2341100*
Just round the corner, same owner, similar dishes, lower prices.

Da Sergio
Piazza San Lorenzo
Classic Florentine *trattoria*; popular with locals. No bookings, cash only.

to be the hub of wine interest in Tuscany, staging exhibitions, debates and tastings. Sadly, it is closed but plans are afoot to reopen it shortly.

FOOD IN FLORENCE

To find food shops in Florence go a few hundred metres out of the centre, where they cluster in abundance. There are *alimentari* (general grocers) and *Pizzicherie* (delicatessen), the Florentine equivalent of the more usual word *gastronomie*.

Florentines also shop at the central market, Mercato San Lorenzo, and the smaller Mercato Sant'Ambrogio (Piazza Ghiberti). The former, enclosed in a fine ironwork building and open every morning (except Sundays) is on two floors and offers a huge selection of fruit and vegetables (including organically grown varieties) upstairs. Downstairs bread, meat, poultry, fish, *salumi*, cheese, eggs, nuts and pulses, even confectionery, are available. The in-house *trattoria*, Da Nerbone, is more than decent too. The smaller Sant'Ambrogio market is useful mainly for its greengrocers, selling produce from small growers from the surrounding countryside.

There is no shortage of places to eat in the centre, if anything the abundance is overwhelming, with scarcely a street food-free, from ice-cream and snack spots to the most

Above *View of Florence with the Santa Croce chapel in the foreground.*
Left *A traditional Florentine* vineria, *very rough and ready, unlike the more modern enoteche.*

sophisticated of restaurants. Caffelatte in Via degli Alfani is good for a mid-morning or afternoon uplift – great coffee with milk and good pastries. Milk and butter are also sold. If in need of a pizza, try Borgo Antico in Piazza Santo Spirito, with its proper wood oven. Drink beer. For a good sandwich on the hoof, stop at the stand of Palmino Pinzauti, Piazza de'Cimatori. In the same square, Birreria Centrale serves good Bavarian beer and a nibble or two to help it down.

It would be unthinkable to visit Florence without indulging in an ice cream. If you want to experience the best home-made flavours and textures go to Vivoli, Via Isole delle Stinche.

DRIVING IN FLORENCE

The rules on access to the city for motorists are unusually complicated. Cars may or may not be allowed in depending on the day of the week, whether or not the car has a catalytic converter and where it comes from. If you can't understand the signs, ask, or you may risk a fine.

Da Ruggero
Via Senese *Tel: 055 220542*
Tightly packed: communal tables and exuberant atmosphere. Typically Tuscan. Best value is house wine.

ENOTECHE

Le Volpi e L'Uva
Piazza dei Rossi
Fun place with good selection of wines by glass and bottle with niblets.
Fuori Porta
Via Monte alle Croci
Tel: 055 2342483
Young, lively. Excellent wine list.
Cantinetta da Verrazzano
Via dei Tavolini *Tel: 055 268590*
Popular wine bar. Wines exclusively from Castello di Verrazzano. Snacks.
Bonatto
Via Gioberti
No tastings, but well stocked shop.
Alessi
Via delle Oche
No tastings, but stock includes a selection of sweetmeats.

FOOD SHOPPING

Bartolozzi
Via V Emanuele.
Superb cheese shop with vast range.
Pegna
Via delle Studio, town centre.
Enticing: eg goose salami, Chinese sauces.
Stenio del Panta
Via Sant'Antonio.
Salumeria specializing in fish.
Leopoldo Procacci
Via Tornabuoni.
An odd mixture of delicacies. Truffle-flavoured bread a speciality.

East of Florence

Heading eastward from Florence towards Pontassieve can prove to be a slow and relatively uninteresting stretch of road. The scenery is not Tuscany's finest and the traffic can be heavy. It is best to keep south of the river and make for Bagno a Ripoli, shortly after which a section of dual carriageway speeds up the journey.

The functional small town of Pontassieve itself has long been a bottle-neck. It marks the confluence of the River Arno as it bends west towards Florence and its tributary, the south-flowing Sieve. Traffic pours in from both these river valleys and from the Casentino to the east (see below). The inevitable snarl-ups give full vent to Italian motoring expressionism and the long-awaited by-pass has been warmly welcomed.

The Arno rises not far from Pontassieve but takes a magnificent horseshoe course, first southward through Poppi and Bibbiena, a sweep known as the Casentino. It is beautiful, more reminiscent of Switzerland than Italy and is famous for its castles and Romanesque abbeys. Neither wine nor olives are produced here.

The river turns on its tail just above Arezzo and flows back to the northwest before meeting the Sieve. In this second stretch, the Val d'Arno Superiore (the Upper Arno Valley), olive cultivation is much in evidence as are flourishing vines. The more southern areas are part of Chianti Colli Aretini, while the middle ranges fall inside Chianti Colli Fiorentini. Only the part closest to the Sieve is within Chianti Rufina, forming a compact zone of extraordinarily high potential.

Above *The faded grandeur of buildings along the Arno (Lungarno) in Florence. From the city, the wine zone of Chianti Rufina can be reached in half an hour.*

Left *Tuscans expend great efforts with flowers to make the outside of their homes colourful and welcoming.*

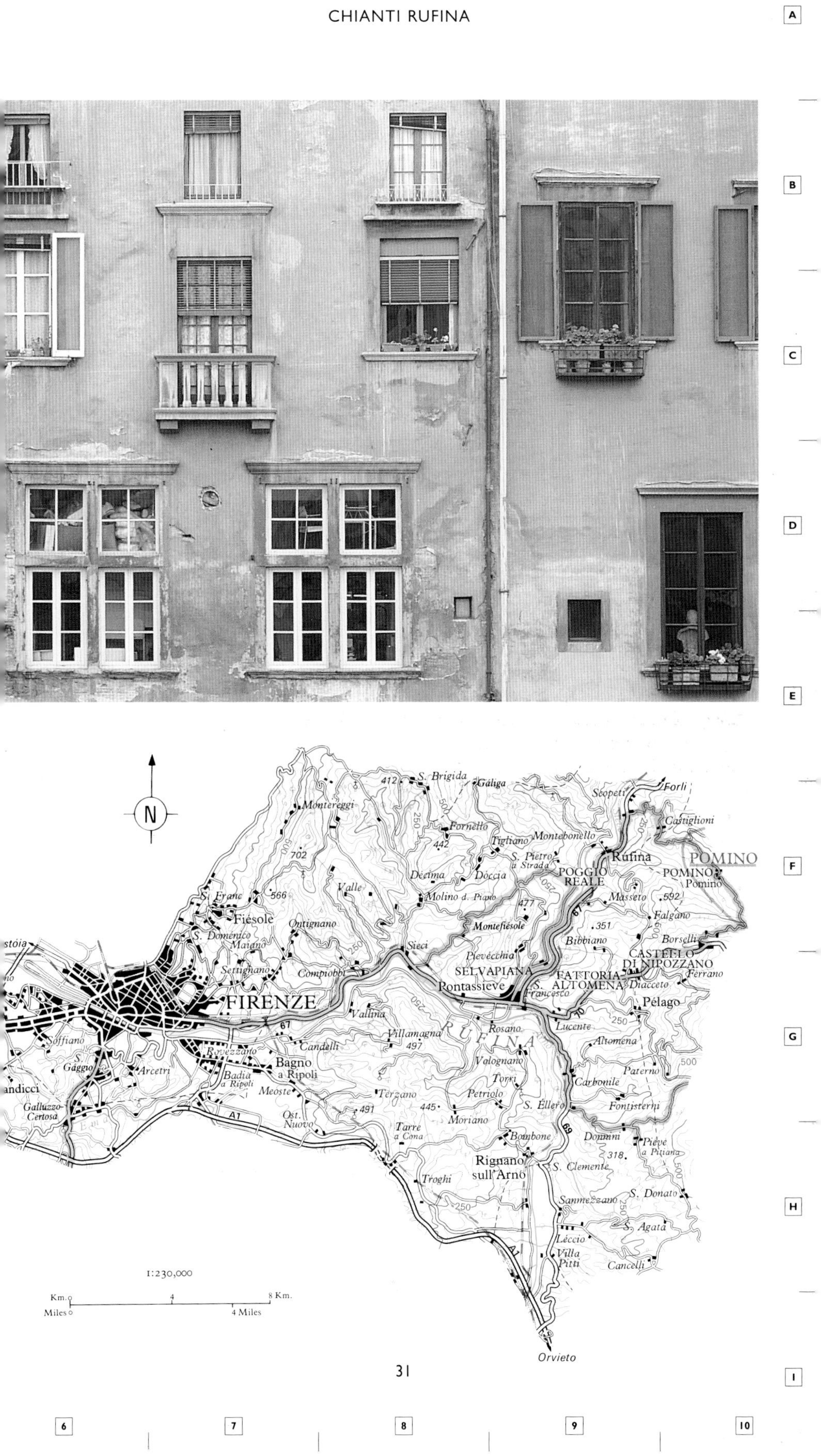

N
S. Brigida
Gàliga
Scopeti
Forlì
Montereggi
Castiglioni
Fornello
Tigliano
Montebonello
S. Pietro a Strada
Rufina
POMINO
POGGIO REALE
POMINO
Pomino
Décima
Dòccia
Valle
Molino d. Piano
Masseto
S. Franc.
Fiésole
Ontignano
Montefiésole
Falgano
S. Domenico
Maiano
Sieci
Bibbiano
Borselli
Pievecchia
CASTELLO DI NIPOZZANO
Settignano
Compiobbi
SELVAPIANA
FATTORIA
Ferrano
Pontassieve
S. Francesco
ALTOMENA
Diacceto
FIRENZE
Vallina
Pélago
Rosano
Lucente
Soffiano
Villamagna
RUFINA
S. Gaggio
Candeli
Altomena
Rovezzano
Arcetri
Bagno a Ripoli
Volognano
Paterno
Badia a Ripoli
Torri
Carbonile
Galluzzo-Certosa
Meoste
Terzano
Petriolo
S. Ellero
Fontisterni
Ost. Nuovo
Moriano
Tarre a Cona
Bombone
Dommi
Pieve a Pitiana
Rignano sull'Arno
S. Clemente
Troghi
S. Donato
Sanmezzano
S. Agata
Léccio
Villa Pitti
Cancelli
Orvieto
A1
1:230,000
Km. 0 4 8 Km.
Miles 0 4 Miles

CHIANTI RUFINA

RECOMMENDED PRODUCERS

Fattoria Selvapiana
Tel: 055 8369848
Francesco Giuntini is related to most of the Tuscan noble families yet remains urbane and down-to-earth. His excellent German is surpassed only by his elegant English. He is certainly charming, probably eccentric and possibly Tuscany's most eligible bachelor. Giuntini owns and runs Selvapiana but trusts the day-to-day winemaking to young Federico Masetti (assisted by consultant Franco Bernabei). Wines: Chianti Rufina; complex, elegant, piercing and long-lasting; cru Bucerchiale defines the better years; Vin Santo; Borro Lastricato, fresh white from Pinot Bianco, Pinot Grigio; latterly Pomino (from Petrognano vineyards). Also top-quality olive oil.

Marchesi di Frescobaldi
Tel: 055 2381400/8311050
Large company run by the Frescobaldi family, vineyards across several estates and numerous wines.

CHIANTI RUFINA

Chianti Rufina straddles the Sieve Valley from Pontassieve upriver to Dicomano. The basic blend of grapes and production criteria are exactly the same as in Chianti Classico but the Rufina wine is firmer, more acidic, more structured and therefore longer-living than most Classico. This is due partly to the sandy calcareous soils and partly to the narrowness of the Sieve Valley, which traps heat by day and loses it by night.

Despite this innate pedigree there are few worthy estates here: just two stand out. The Marchesi di Frescobaldi, with over 500ha of vine and numerous estates, dominates the scenery but Fattoria Selvapiana has the more finely tuned wines. Other estates are slowly emerging: Bossi, for example, and the once-defunct Spalletti which is being revived. Yet some vines look surprisingly run-down and uncared for. Progress may have been hampered by confusion between the area Rufina (accented on the first syllable) and the big Chianti Classico house Ruffino, but a residual malaise still hovers over parts of the zone. The recently reformed Rufina Consorzio is working hard to overcome the zone's profile and, among other initiatives, encourages member estates to welcome visitors gladly.

Above left *Spring in Tuscany brings a riot of flowers.*
Above *Tuscan bread, firm but unsalted, is a staple.*

Pontassieve is the best starting point for any round trip. For a sight of the right-bank estates, cross the river at Pontassieve and follow it to Montebonello (in effect a continuation of the left-bank town of Rufina). Turn inland to San Pietro a Strada and Monterifrassine, continuing to join the main road from Florence to Pontassieve just below Sieci. The first estate you see is Fattoria di Basciano to the right, with its renovated medieval tower; then, on the left, Villa di Vetrice with its 12th-century tower. After Monterifrassine, Fattoria di Lavacchio appears, followed by Tenuta di Bossi, a 15th-century villa, both on the left. From time to time, as the road curves, the Torre di Arcone, a tall medieval tower, is visible in the middle distance. Medieval and Renaissance splendours are certainly not lacking in this part of Tuscany.

The heart of Rufina and its two most important estates lie south of the Sieve. From Pontassieve head south along the Upper Arno, following the railway, and within a minute or two Vallombrosa and Passo della Consuma are signposted to the left. Turn off to see Frescobaldi's Castello di Nipozzano (a few minutes' along on the left) or explore the Casentino; otherwise keep going for a circuit which, in a couple of leisurely hours, will take you through the essence of Rufina.

From Castello di Nipozzano, the major estate, Chianti Rufina Riserva crus Nipozzano and highly rated Montesodi, super-Tuscan Mormoreto; from Remole, Chianti Rufina Remole; from Tenuta di Pomino, Pomino red and white plus oaked white Pomino Il Benefizio; and many more. Also owns Castelgiocondo estate in Montalcino.

Tenuta di Bossi
Pontassieve *Tel: 055 8317830*
Up-and-coming estate. *Agriturismo.*

HOTELS

Both Pontassieve and Rufina have hotels, the **Moderno** and **La Speranza** respectively. But since both towns are rather dreary, stay elsewhere if possible.

Villa Pitiana
Donnini
Tel: 055 860259
A magnificent complex comprising opulent hotel, *agriturismo* apartments and restaurant attached to the cloisters of an ancient Vallombrosano monastery. Fabulous views over the Arno to Chianti Classico. Swimming pool. Food traditional but refined – probably the best in the Rufina area. Not over-priced; excellent value. Hotel open April to October. Restaurant open weekends only during winter.

Below and right *Fattoria Selvapiana's cellars and vineyards are more elegant than their sales points. They also produce some of Tuscany's finest olive oil.*

The area is liberally dotted with medieval houses. The more important habitations were necessarily fortressed. But the *case coloniche*, simple workers' houses, are fabulous in their own way. They have a satisfying solidity and an elegance of design that is hard to match and yet meld effortlessly into the countryside. The first to appear on the right, with their soft arches, are absolutely typical. The first vineyards, on the left, are leased by the estate Castello di Trebbio (a 13th-century castle at northerly Santa Brigida, physically outside Rufina). Those that follow reflect Rufina's downside, in vines that are not particularly well tended, whose grapes are often sent to the Cantina Sociale. The imposing Castello Volognano then emerges across the river, and, in front, on a clear day the steep slopes of Chianti Classico's Gaiole (see p62).

Head left for Vallombrosa at Sant'Ellero. The tower on the left marks a small former monastery which is now a privately-owned house. Within a matter of seconds, the road begins to rise and the scenery becomes more wooded and very beautiful. This area, spanning the ridge between the Val d'Arno Superiore and Vallombrosa, is called the

Pratomagno. Again, the buildings are a mixture of medieval and Renaissance architecture. You are already outside the Chianti Rufina district and vines disappear into the distance.

A side-road to the right leads to the Pieve a Pitiana, one of a number of simple but powerful Romanesque churches found along the Upper Arno, and also to an optional (long) extension to the tour along the 'Road of the Seven Bridges', so-called because it hops over each of the Upper Arno's tributaries. Alternatively, the driveway to the Villa Pitiana on the left is a real gem. Rising up to Tosi brings views back down over Rufina and its ampitheatre of olive and vine. Tosi is dominated by artisanal wooden furniture-making.

From there follow the sign to Saltino. Reaching the Pian di Melusa, you are surrounded by a thick pine forest: the scene looks distinctly more Tyrolean than Tuscan. The forest, owned by monks until 1860, was controlled by the Forestry Commission until 1949, when it was partially restored to its original owners. A combination of fir, pine, and beech trees keeps the soil neutral and, even during winter, there is a stunning mix of dark green and vivid copper colours lining the road.

At 1,000m the road bends sharply, and suddenly, surprisingly, the monastery of Vallombrosa appears ahead. Dense forest interspersed with gushing waterfalls lines the route down to Consuma, where the countryside opens out and vistas of vines and olives return. Here Chianti Rufina is temporarily interrupted by Pomino.

AGRITURISMO

The following estates have *agriturismo* apartments. See also under Recommended Producers.

Fattoria di Petrognano
Tel: 055 8318812
Wine, housed in ancient underground cellars, is made by Selvapiana. Own trattoria. Closed October to Easter.

Fattoria di Basciano
Montebonello *Tel: 055 8397034*

Fattoria il Frantoio
Dicomano *Tel: 055 8397886*

Az Agr Capiteto
Acone *Tel: 055 8361600*
With swimming pool

Soggiorno al Lago
Vicchio *Tel: 055 8448638*
With swimming, horse riding, mountain biking and other activities.

RESTAURANTS

Vicolo del Contento
Castelfranco di Sopra
Tel 055 9149277
Castelfranco is a 15th-century village half-way along the Upper Arno which, unusually, was built to a grid system rather than growing haphazardly. The restaurant is smart with modern, high-class Tuscan cuisine. Huge pan-Italian wine list. Closed Monday, Tuesday. Quite expensive but good value.

Gliaccaniti
Pratovecchio
Tel: 0575 583345
Convenient for those touring the Casentino. Small, comfortable; traditional ingredients, modern touch. Broad selection of Tuscan wines. Mid-priced. Closed Tuesday.

Osteria di Paterna
Tel: 055 977514
Opens weekends only. Cash only. Friendly and well run, on a cooperative mixed farming estate. Drink the estate's own wine.

Main picture *Overlooking Pomino and Chianti Rufina. Most of the Pomino valley belongs to the Frescobaldi, which has vineyards across several estates.*
Below left *Frescobaldi's coat-of-arms. The family has over six centuries of winemaking experience.*

POMINO

Pomino abuts and slightly overlaps Chianti Rufina. The zone centres on Pomino village and is edged by the Rufina stream, which runs into the Sieve at Rufina itself. It is one of Italy's smallest DOC zones and was also one of the first to be denominated, in 1716.

In the mid-19th century Marchese Vittorio degli Albizi planted French grape varieties here, and today's wines respect that tradition. The white is made mainly from Pinot Bianco and Chardonnay, the red has Cabernet, Merlot and sometimes Pinot Nero mixed with the normal Sangiovese. Until recently there was only the wine of Frescobaldi, from their newly planted Tenuta di Pomino estate, but Fattoria Selvapiana has newly entered the fray, renting vineyards from the old Fattoria di Petrognano with the enterprise and the wines are causing quite a stir.

Consuma, where the Vallombrosa road meets the Pontassieve–Casentino road, marks the furthest extent of the Pomino zone. Turn left, towards Pontassieve, and the road skirts its boundary. The smart Renaissance house on the right is Spedaletto, one of Frescobaldi's many villas. After a brief wooded stretch there is a panoramic view to the right

Il Canto del Maggio
Tel: 055 9705147
Unusual: refined trattoria! Traditional basis with imaginative touches. Eating place of the literati. Small but good wine selection.

PLACES OF INTEREST

Villa Poggio Reale
The Ufficio Cultura of the Comune di Rufina.
Tel: 055 839611I
It is said that this 16th-century villa was designed by Michelangelo but it was probably the work of his followers. It has been carefully restored to house the Chianti Rufina museum of vine and wine. View by appointment.

Monastery of Vallombrosa
The Vallombrosano was an order of monks derived from the Benedictine. This commanding building hugged by pine forests is high in the Pratomagno. Remains of the kitchen garden and trout lake lead to the crested entrance. The church is always open. The abbey can be seen by guided tours at 10.30am Tuesdays and Fridays between June and September.

FOOD SHOPPING

Cooperative Il Forteto
To the right, heading up the Sieve between Dicomano and Vicchio. Youngsters recovering from drug-related and other problems produce and sell superb sheep and goats' cheeses (the *Pecorino* is wonderful), *salumeria*, honey and other preserves. The produce is also available in Florence's San Lorenzo market.

Fabrizio Fabbrini
Terranuova Bracciolini
Butcher famed for meat from Chianina cattle and cured meats.

Cooperative Agricola Valdarnese
L'Osteria di Paterna
Wide range of agricultural products all organically grown.

Top *Casks of Vin Santo mature in Frescobaldi's cellars in Pomino.*
Right *Vineyards surround the villa of Selvapiana, producer of complex and elegant Chianti Rufina.*

FAIRS

Bacco Artigiano
Rufina: Last week of September, Thursday to Sunday. Exhibition and sale of wines and local crafts.

over the whole Pomino valley – and a convenient lay-by from which to survey it. After Borselli the Romanesque church of Tosina appears on the left. From the church (which has a pretty cloister) there are more good views: with the Rufina stream snaking into the Sieve valley.

Just before Pomino village, the long, low house to the left is one of Frescobaldi's most important villas and reception venues. Vin Santo ages in casks behind its windows. The main attraction of Pomino itself is the Pieve di San Bartolomeo. Just outside is a rare example of old-fashioned vine culture: vines trained over maple shoots.

A few minutes' down from the village is the Fattoria di Petrognano. Further along on the right, just before the Pomino gives way again to Chianti Rufina, is Pomino's third Romanesque church, the Pieve di Castiglioni.

RETURN TO CHIANTI RUFINA

After Castiglioni you are back in the Chianti Rufina zone and, within a few minutes, right down on the Sieve Valley floor. Turn left and head back through Rufina itself, which is not the prettiest of towns. The Torre di Arcone punctuates the right bank while ahead rises the imposing sight of Poggio Reale. A short distance before Pontassieve there is a terracotta display on the left and an unmarked lane. This is the driveway up to the Fattoria Selvapiana, veering off over a level crossing. As the lane rises it quickly becomes olive-lined and vine-circled and the actual entrance to the Villa is far more imposing.

PASSO DEL MURAGLIONE

An optional extra and a glorious way to spend a morning (when the sun is in the right direction), especially if the weather is clear, is a visit to the Passo del Muraglione. Over 900m above sea-level, this is the highest peak on the old road over the Apennines, the road used between Tuscany and the Adriatic before the advent of motorways. There is a tall stretch of wall (the *Muraglione*) in the middle of the road, reputedly built as a wind-break to stop carriages from being blown off. There is not much at the top apart from the wall and the wind but it is the journey that counts. Take the road along the Sieve past Rufina to Dicomano and there fork to the right. Gradually the road begins to snake upwards and at every third or fourth twist you get increasingly magnificent views of central Tuscany – right across Chianti Classico.

Chianti Classico

Diverse as Tuscany's scenery is, it is hardly surprising that the entire region has become associated with its most famous part, the land of Chianti Classico. Its 70,000 hectares of hilly land contain some of the most breathtaking views in Europe. There is such variety that it is almost worth getting lost, although efficient signposting makes it difficult to wander aimlessly within the zone. Bumpy tracks apparently heading off to nowhere almost always emerge onto one of the asphalted roads that saunter from village to village.

Chianti Classico can be reached in just a few minutes from Florence to the north, Siena to the south and the San Donato exit from the Florence–Siena superstrada to the west. For just a glimpse of Chianti Classico's splendours, take the Chiantigiana, the main north–south road through the area. Much would be missed, though, if you restricted yourself to that.

The district has long been called Chianti, the name of the wines followed. The name had such cachet that when wine laws were first promulgated in the 1960s, producers in the surrounding districts grabbed their opportunity to share the benefits. As a result the wine area 'Chianti' stretches from north of Pistoia to south of Montalcino and from Livorno to Arezzo. The real, historical zone therefore took on the appendix Classico, to indicate the classic heartland. The rest was split into sub-districts, which, with the exception of the small zones of Chianti Rufina and Chianti Montalbano, followed provincial lines: Chianti Colli Senesi, those from the province of Pisa, Chianti Colline Pisane and so on. Many would like the name Chianti once more to be restricted to the Classico area only, which could happen. At least a new revision to the wine law treats the Classico separately.

Chianti, the wine, is red, its character deriving from the difficult but rewarding Sangiovese grape – difficult because it easily produces good wines, only skillful handling can make it great, and rewarding because the wines reflect the diversity of site on which it is grown in an infinite variety of complex and subtle variations.

A geological map of the area reveals a complex pattern of soil outcrops but the wines come from the esteemed lime-

Left *Vineyards, olive groves, pine forest and cypresses – typical Chianti countryside.*

Above *Volpaia, with its red rooftops and hill-top position, epitomises a typical Tuscan village.*

Bologna
Ugnano
FIRENZE
Pisa
Stagno
Lastra a Signa
Calcinaia
Rovezzano
Soffiano
S. Gaggio
Arcetri
Badia a Ripoli
Meoste
S. Martino alla Palma
Scandicci
Galluzzo Certosa
Ost. Nuovo
Bricoli
Marliano
Roveta
Mosciano
Grassina
Antella
S. Donato in Collina
Inno
Sorg
S. Paolo a. Mosc.
Bàlatro
Marciola
COLLI FIORENTINI
Càrcheri
la Sughera
S. Andrea a Morgiano
Tavarnuzze
Montebuoni
S. Vincenzo a Torri
S. Michele a Torri
Chiesa-nuova
Capannuccia
Pgio. di Firenze 694
Ròmola
CONTI SERRISTORI
Campo d. Ugolino
S. Andrea in P.
M. Masso 467
Terme di Firenze
Impruneta
Cerbàia
PALAZZO AL BOSCO
S. Stéfano a Tizzana
S. Polo in Chianti
M. Muro 634
Talente
Cigliano
PASIGNANO
ANTINORI
VITIANO
Montagnana
Montegufoni
Linari
Argiano
Strada in Chianti
Fezzana
la Ripa
S. Casciano in Val di Pesa
il Ferrone
298
Poppiano
Calcinaia
FIRENZE
M. Moggino 730
MONTEPALDI
LE CORTI
Montespèrtoli
QUERCETO E SANTA LUCIA
Chiocchio
Cintoia
Castellina
Lucignano
Mercatale
TERCIONA
CASTELLI GREVEPESA
NOZZOLE
S. Pietro in Mercato
S. Angelo
Passo dei Pecorai
San Pancrazio
Aliano
le Quattro Strade
GABBIANO
S. STEFANO
Carpignalle
S. Lorenzo
Fornacette
Bargino
le Bolle
Celle
250
S. Giusto a Montalbino
Montefiridolfi
CASTELLO DI UZZANO
S. Gaudenzio a Campoli
VERRAZZANO
Rugliana
Tresanti
Lucardo
422
CALCINAIA
SOCIETA ESPORTAZIONE VINI AFFINI
Maggiano
VICCHIOMAGGIO
S. Donato
S. Michele a Polvereto
S.M. Macerata
S. Martino a Maiano
S. Gaudenzio a Rubalta
407
Romita
Fàbbrica
CASTELLO DI MONTEFIORALLE
Greve in Chianti
M. Domini 747
Fiano
Badia a Passignano
Noce
M. Fili 554
Monte-fioralle
Lucolena
il Pino
Marcialla
Sambuca
Nebbiano
Pta. 526
Pernano
Vitigliano
Corti
Torsoli
Pisa
Morrocco
CASENUOVE
Canònica
Travarnelle Val di Pesa
MONTAGLIARI
Càsole
Mte. S. Michele
892
Certaldo
Agliena
S.M. a Bagnano
Magliano
MONTAGLIARI E CASTELLINUZZA
LA QUERCIA
Lamole
Barberino Val d'Elsa
Panzano in Chianti
la Villa
LE PILE E LAMOLE
Sciano
Petrognano
Tignano
S. Donato
SICELLE
Sicelle
Campana
VIGNAMAGGIO
M. Querciabella 845
S. Donnino
Mad. di Pietracupa
Piazza
Pieve di Panzano
S. Vito
LA PESANELLA
429
S. Benedetto
S. Filippo
Cortine
Lucarelli
Volpaia
Vico d'Elsa
S. Appiano
Piecorto
Castelvecchi
CASTELLO DI VOLPAIA
TENUTA RICAVO' (Hotel)
Ricavo
Ulignano
PANERETTA
222
Linari
MONSANTO
CAMPOMAGGIO
SANTEDAME
Pgio. Cavallari
VIGNALE
Gavignano
Cedda
GODENANO SECONDO
648
la Croce
Pgio. la Croce 633
Radda in Chianti
Casàglia
MELINI
S. Agnese
632
FRATENILLI
ORMANNI
S. Giusto in Salcio
S. Gimignano
CONSORZIO AGRARIO PROVINCIALE DI SIENA
578
Castellina in Chianti
CASTELLINA
Poggibonsi
Luco
SIENA
S. Lucchese
VILLAROSA
S. Lucia
250
Arbia
525
Monti
Bibbiano
BIBBIANO
FONTERUTOLI
Fonterutoli
S. Fedele
Montauto
Castiglioni
Lecchi
LE PIAZZE
620
Colle di Val d'Elsa
CERNA
LILLIANO
CAMPALLI
500
FRANCESCO BERTOLLI
Vagliagli
Volterra
68
S. Leonino
MOCENNI
LODOLINE
Petròio
CASALINO
COLLI SENESI
S. Antonio al Bosco
CASTELLO DI RENCINE
AGRICOLT CHIANTI GE
Busona
Lornano
Fornacella
Quercegrossa
Monteriggioni
Corsignano
Badesse
Poggiolo
Basciano
Pontignano
CASTELL CERRETO CATIGNANO
1:230,000
Km. 0 4 8 Km.
Miles 0 4 Miles
Uopini
S. Dalmazio
S. Giova
le Tolfe
408
Grosseto
Larniano
Vignano
Tuorlo
Siena
A1
2
3
222
A B C D E F G H I
1 2 3 4 5

Right *The well known* Gallo Nero *(black cockerel) symbol of the Conzorzio del Marchio Storico-Chianti-Classico, which adorns all its members' bottles.*

stone *alberese,* clay-schist *galestro* or, in the higher areas, sandstone. The highest vineyards top 600m, the lowest are around 250m and, although southwest- or southeast-facing slopes are favoured, vines grow on many aspects.

Starry as Sangiovese is, it is not the sole constituent of Chianti. Small quantities of other grapes are also included. In the mid-19th century the Barone Bettino Ricasoli laid down his formula for the wine, which included the red grape Canaiolo, and the white grapes Trebbiano and Malvasia. The aim, however, was a light, easy-drinking wine, not today's fuller more serious bottles. In 1984, Chianti was up-graded to DOCG. The regulation Sangiovese content was increased to 75–90 percent. Now, a new revision will finally allow Chianti Classico to contain unsullied Sangiovese.

Those who do want 100 percent Sangiovese have, until now, either cheated or, more usually, made another wine beside their Chianti Classico.

Chianti Classico

—·—·—	Provincia boundary
▬	Boundary of DOCG Chianti Classico area
RUFINA	Other Chianti zones
POMINO	Other DOC
CASALINO	Important cellars
☐	Vineyards
☐	Areas not legally Chianti
☐	Woods
250	Contour interval 50 metres
▬	Wine route

These wines, often a producer's best, have been dubbed 'super-Tuscans', reflecting their quality and erstwhile lack of classification. Other super-Tuscans are more experimental, often blending Sangiovese with Cabernet Sauvignon. (A small proportion of Cabernet is sometimes used in Chianti anyway, to give a more rounded, fruity style.) There are non-traditional whites, too, often from Chardonnay or, sometimes, Sauvignon/Sémillon blends and sometimes aged in *barrique* or, more commonly *botti*. These innovative wines will gradually be absorbed into the new wine law (see p17).

The people of Chianti have long been aware of differences in the style between the area's communes: San Casciano, Greve and its sub-zone Panzano, Barberino Val d'Elsa, Castellina, Radda, Gaiole and Castelnuovo Berardenga. Now quantifying and describing these individual commune styles is increasingly important.

Below *Shady, winding streets and tiled roofs are typical of towns and villages throughout Tuscany.*

Above left *A tiny roadside chapel near Badia a Passignano in Chianti Classico.*
Top *Fresh tomatoes form the basis of much Tuscan cuisine.*
Above *Concrete vats have now been replaced on many estates by the more efficient stainless steel.*

There is also research into the best clones, rootstocks and planting densities for each site as most vineyards will shortly be due for replanting. In preparation, the Chianti Classico Consorzio has engaged on a research project, Chianti Classico 2000, to ensure the highest quality in the future.

A *consorzio* is a voluntary generic body set up to protect its members' interests. In the Classico zone there are two. The Consorzio del Chianti Classico is the legal watchdog, checking by tasting, analyses and vineyard and cellar visits that wines are in line with regulations. It also hands out the pinky-purple DOCG neck labels that adorn all satisfactory wines. Anyone producing Chianti Classico needs to belong. The second is the Conzorzio del Marchio Storico-Chianti Classico, the promotions and marketing body. The black cockerel (*gallo nero*) is its well-known symbol. Its title used to be the Consorzio del Gallo Nero, and still is in Italy. But a court case brought by the American wine company Gallo successfully banned the use of the word abroad.

The local white grapes are Trebbiano, Toscano and Malvasia, which give light, fresh wine. Producers in southern Classico use DOC Bianco Val d'Arbia, this also covers whites made south of the Classico, near Siena. These white grapes also make the exciting flagship Vin Santo.

SAN CASCIANO

RECOMMENDED PRODUCERS

Machiavelli
Tel: 0577 989001
Cellars run under the site of Niccolò Macchiavelli's home. Soft wines.

Conti Serristori
Tel: 0577 989001
Conti Serristori and Machiavelli (above) are both part of the large merchant house Melini.

Fattoria La Loggia
Tel: 055 8244288
Smallish, founded in 1427, with vineyards surrounding an ancient fortress. Produces super-Tuscan Nearco (Sangiovese/Cabernet), Vin Santo, sparkling wines and others as well as Chianti Classico. Olive oil. *Agriturismo.*

Antinori
(See also Cantinetta Antinori in Florence.) *Tel: 055 23595*
Over 600 years old, in family hands and Italy's best-known and reputed company. Numerous estates in Tuscany (and adjacent Umbria). Carefully crafted wines of great appeal. Many produced including Chianti Classico, Badia a Passignano, Peppoli, Santa Cristina, plus famed super-Tuscans Tignanello (Sangiovese/Cabernet) and Solaia (mainly Cabernet).

Castello di Gabbiano
Good Chianti and Sangiovese super-Tuscans. Quality steadily improving.

HOTEL

Antica Posta
See opposite.

San Casciano

From the Firenze Certosa junction off the Firenze-Siena superstrada and just south of Florence, within five minutes you can be rising into the first hills of Chianti Classico. Sant'Andrea in Percussina marks not only the first glimpses of vines but, symbolically, the offices of the Chianti Classico Consorzio. It may be worth a short stop to pick up their detailed map, which is as useful for general touring as it is for finding the Consorzio member estates.

The offices are on the site of the old house of Machiavelli. The Machiavelli museum is opposite. However – this is Italy remember – the museum is run by the owners of the adjacent restaurant (see right), so, to visit it you need to turn up around lunch or dinner time, otherwise it is closed. The Machiavelli and Conti Serristori estates are just next door.

San Casciano, a couple of minutes' further along the road, is a pleasant enough small town. There are a few estates to the northwest along the road to Cerbaia, but the more important ones are in the opposite direction. Generally, though, San Casciano, with its white and yellow limestone soils, is more important for olive oil production than for wine, and olive trees dominate the scenery. If you look carefully, many will appear to have oddly slim branches sprouting from aged, thick trunks. These are the regrowths from the dire frosts of 1985 (see p20).

Above *San Casciano is a pleasant town and home to one of Italy's top restaurants, La Tenda Rosso.*
Left Pappardelle con ragu, *a pasta dish in* trattorie.
Top right and right *Olive groves around San Casciano. The area is the most important in Classico for olive oil.*

For an idea of the life of the Tuscan nobility in the past, take a look at the Fattoria delle Corti Corsini, just on the right, a kilometre along the road to Mercatale. The solid, imposing-looking building has both cellars and an important *frantoio* (oil-extraction plant). A few minutes' further on, it is worth taking a short detour right to Montefiridolfi. There, swing right to see Fattoria La Loggia, an estate with over five centuries of history, or left for a glimpse of where Antinori's much-admired Santa Cristina is made. Back in Mercatale, go through the small town and shortly afterwards there is a crossroads. Turn left (signposted Greve) for Castello di Gabbiano and the Castelgreve cooperative winery. Bear in mind that the road is unmade and not much fun if the weather is wet. Instead, go right (towards Panzano) and the road leads upwards through woodland, vines and olive groves. San Pietro a Sillano off to the left is a tranquil, pretty, privately owned church. But from here onwards you are in the commune of Greve.

RESTAURANTS

San Casciano has plenty of good places to eat. It is so close to Florence that Florentines often drive out rather than struggle through the city. Other restaurants listed follow the wine route.

Antica Posta
Tel: 055 820116
Non-traditional but delightful. Light, flavoursome food relying on the best local ingredients. Well chosen wines. Also a hotel. Closed Mondays.

La Tenda Rossa
Cerbaia *Tel: 055 826132*
One of Italy's top restaurants. Super-smart, very good indeed, huge wine list but costly. Closed Wednesday and Thursday lunchtime.

L'Albergaccio
Tel: 055 828471
Sant'Andrea in Percussina
Simple *trattoria*-style food. Also houses the Machiavelli museum. Closed Mondays.

Da Nello
San Casciano *Tel: 055 820163*
Hearty, flavoursome, traditional food with one or two flourishes, relying on local, seasonal ingredients. Decent wine selection. Closed Wednesday evening and Thursdays. Best at lunchtime.

FOOD SHOPPING

Cooperative La Ginestra
(loc Barsino, via Pergolato 3)
Full range of local produce, all organically produced.

Greve and Panzano

Of all Chianti Classico's commune centres, Greve is the liveliest. The hub is the the central piazza, and the highlight the *macelleria* (butchers) Falorni, which specializes in everything from *cinghiale* (wild boar) products. To emphasize the point a (stuffed) wild boar stands guard outside. Just along from here is a small crafts shop selling among other things, wine bottle stoppers adorned with Chianti's famed black cockerel. There are also a couple of *enoteche*.

Practically all Greve's estates are within 15 minutes' drive of the town; most are closer. Arriving from San Casciano, the first signed junction to the left after the church of San Pietro di Sillano leads in via Montefioralle. This is a superb medieval but Etruscan-looking village perched on a hill-top. Before taking that left turn, however, you could detour straight ahead for just half a kilometre to see the smallish but highly esteemed estate Vecchie Terre di Montefili.

Leaving Greve northward is the Chiantigiana, the 'major' road that winds right through Chianti Classico from south of Florence to Siena. Within five minutes you pass the estates Villa Calcinaia, Castello di Verrazzano and Castello Vicchiomaggio, on the left, on classic *alberese* limestone soil.

Eastward from Greve the road is slower. The soil here has more sandstone and there are fewer estates, but follow the road towards Figline Valdarno and you will see Riseccoli,

GREVE

RECOMMENDED PRODUCERS

Vecchie Terre di Montefili
Tel: 055 853739
Small estate with acclaimed wines, notably Chianti Classico cru Anfiteatro Riserva and super-Tuscan Bruno di Rocca (Sangiovese/Cabernet).

Villa Calcinaia
Tel: 055 854008
Owned by the Capponi family since the 16th century. Well styled, clean wines. Direct sales.

Castello di Verrazzano
Tel: 055 854243
Originally an Etruscan settlement; wine certainly produced here in the 12th century. Set high over the Greve Valley with excellent views of the

vineyards. The estate was bought by the Verrazzano family in the 7th century (a descendant of whom, born in 1485, landed at New York and discovered much of the USA's east coast). Carefully made wines, predominantly Chianti Classico. Warm hospitality.

Castello Vicchiomaggio
Tel: 055 854079
Impressive, four-square building of medieval origin. Mid-sized. Tightly knit, stylish wines. Chianti Classico Riserva Petri and Prima Vigna top the range. Also Chianti Classico Boscorotondo and super-Tuscans Ripa della More (Sangiovese/Cabernet) and Ripa delle Mimose (Chardonnay). *Agriturismo*: preference given to wine-lovers. Banqueting rooms. Tastings at cost.

Castello di Querceto and Carpineto. Heading south from Greve brings you onto a cool, wooded stretch of the Chiantigiana. Either turn to Panzano, or fork left after leaving Greve and turn immediately right onto a circular estate-hopping route which takes you past Savignola Paolina, owned by the Fabbri family for 200 years, Vignamaggio and 16th-century Castellinuzza. La Doccia, in the Cinuzzi family since the 16th century, follows, then Filetta and the castle of Lamole (officially Lamole di Lamole, to distinguish it from the eponymous village), one of Greve's major fortresses.

Turning right shortly after passing Lamole (the estate) brings you into Panzano territory.

Riseccoli
Tel: 055 853598
Bought by sculptor Romano Romanelli at the turn of the century. Small, well aspected vineyard. Olive oil. *Agriturismo.*

Castello di Querceto
Tel: 055 8549064
Over 470m above sea-level, overlooking the valley and strategically important. Lombard origins, destroyed at the end of the 15th century, later rebuilt in similar style as a villa. Further restorations followed. Over a dozen firmly structured wines led by Chianti Classico Il Picchio; super-Tuscans La Corte (Sangiovese) and Querciolaia. *Agriturismo.*

Carpineto
Tel: 055 8549062.
Comparatively new estate with a wide range of carefully made, well balanced reliable wines from other grapes and areas of Tuscany as well as the mainstay, Chianti Classico.

Querciabella
Tel: 055 853834
Good Chianti Classico and super-Tuscan Camartina (Sangiovese/ Cabernet Sauvignon) Pleasant tasting room, tastings by appointment.

Vignamaggio
Greve *Tel: 055 853559*
Carefully restored 15th-century villa with beautiful Italian garden. Mona Lisa was born here. 160ha estate of which 32ha under vine. Wine has been produced here since at least 1400. After a weak patch, wines now regaining high status, especially Chianti Classico Mona Lisa and super-Tuscan Gherardino (Sangiovese). Olive oil. *Agriturismo.*

Lamole
Tel: 055 9501005
22ha of well sited vines.

Far left *Falorni, the Greve butcher, specialising in boar.*
Main picture *On the way to Greve from San Casciano is the fortress of Castello di Gabbiano, overlooking the Greve valley.*
Top *A harvest scene in Chianti. Today openwork boxes are more commonly used to carry the grapes.*

Right *Panzano, where a moderate climate and favorable soil result in some of the most refined Chianti Riserva.*

PANZANO

RECOMMENDED PRODUCERS

Montagliari
Tel: 055 483819
Owned by the Cappelli family since 1730. Medium-sized estate. Lively, cheerful atmosphere. Good wines. Unusual dry Vin Santo. *Agriturismo.* Own *trattoria* (see p51).

Cennatoio
Tel: 055 852134
Smallish, hospitable eight hectare estate. Good wines.

Castello dei Rampolla
Tel: 055 852001
36ha of fairly high-altitude vineyard. Highly rated super-Tuscan Sammarco (mainly Cabernet) is their pride but Chianti Classico also fine.

La Massa
Tel: 055 852701
Owned by lively Neapolitans. Wines improving annually: particularly good in poor years. 12-bed villa available.

Vignole
Tel: 055 592025
Very welcoming; good wines.

Le Masse di San Leolino
Tel: 055 852144
Owned by an Englishman, Norman Bain. Produces little but very good wine: elegant and firm.

Fontodi
Tel: 055 852005
Mid-sized estate. Superb wines. Flaccianello delle Pieve one of the best 100% Sangiovese super-Tuscans in Chianti. Chianti Classico and cru Vigna del Sorbo both stunning.

Il Poggiolino
Sambuca Val di Pesa
Tel: 055 8071635
Well worth a longish detour to visit this friendliest of estates (Sambuca is signed right just after entering Greve commune). Open, rounded Chianti.

PANZANO

Panzano is officially a sub-commune of Greve but it is usually treated as if it were a commune in its own right. It is much calmer and quieter than Greve, having comparatively few people pounding its steep, narrow streets and it is one of Chianti's prettiest villages.

At the top of the hill is a well cared for church with a warden who just loves to get his face into photographs. The real draw to the village, however, is a *macelleria,* a butcher's shop a few paces down from the church, known simply as Dario's. He draws customers from as far afield as Florence and they come for the quality of his meat (Dario rears his own sheep) but also for his ready-prepared cuts, which can cater for smart dinners, large parties or even picnics. It is

even one of the few butchers where classical music drifts across the counter from a stereo system.

Coming into Panzano from the Chiantigiana you pass Montagliari; coming in from Lamole you see Cennatoio. Once through the village, take a brief jaunt onwards, forking left onto an unmade road. A lane to the left brings you to Castello di Rampolla; an equally uncomfortable track takes you to La Massa and Vignole. Turn back to Panzano, go through the village once more and head southwest (towards Castellina). After a couple of minutes Le Masse di San Leolino appears on the left followed by the magnificent Fontodi, the last of the Panzano estates.

Looking back, you can see the village perched up to the right behind you.

HOTELS

Albergo del Chianti
Greve
Tel: 055 853763
With swimming pool. Mid-priced.

Il Verrazzano
Greve
Tel: 055 853189
Simple pensione. Also traditional trattoria.

Villa Sangiovese
Panzano
Tel: 055 852461
Attractive and comfortable with swimming pool. Closed in winter.

RESTAURANTS

Il Vescovino
Panzano
Tel: 055 852464
Traditional ingredients, elegantly prepared. Seats outside in summer.

Trattoria del Montagliari
Panzano
Tel: 055 852184
On the estate premises: popular with locals and Florentines. A fire blazes in winter in the long, rectangular room furnished with dark wooden benches. The food is hearty, strongly meat-based and full of flavour. Portions are large. Full use is made of local and seasonal ingredients. Not expensive. Closed Mondays.

ENOTECHE

La Cantinetta
Greve

Bottega del Chianti Classico
Greve

Enoteca del Chianti Classico
Panzano

Note: the Bar del Gallo Nero is not an enoteche, but an ordinary bar.

SPECIAL EVENTS

Rassegna del Chianti
Greve
A celebration of local produce. A large market in the piazza sells wine, oil, vinegars, honey and related products. End of September to beginning of October.

Barberino

BARBERINO

RECOMMENDED PRODUCERS

Isole e Olena
Tel: 055 8072763
Some of the best wines in Tuscany. Owner Paolo de Marchi produces beautiful, intensely fruity wines of great character. In the vineyard he is painstakingly recreating terraces on a well aspected site of prime *galestro* soil. Wines include Chianti Classico; Cepparello, acclaimed super-tuscan 100% Sangiovese; Vin Santo; Syrah, Cabernet Sauvignon, Chardonnay.

Le Filigare
Tel: 055 8072796
Small estate with *agriturismo*

Villa Francesca
Tel: 055 8072849
Tiny estate with *agriturismo*, its own restaurant and a recently built hotel.

Casa Sola
Tel: 055 8075028
Large estate with *agriturismo*, tennis courts and a swimming pool. Also produces Vin Santo and olive oil.

Casa Emma
Tel: 055 8072859
A hill-top stone house surrounded by vineyard. Wine receiving plaudits.

Fattoria La Ripa
Tel: 055 8072948
Agriturismo. Also raises lobsters!

Fattoria Monsanto
Tel: 055 8075131
Quality wines, long ageing potential.

Castello della Paneretta
A 15th-century castle restored at the end of the 17th century. *Agriturismo*. Group tastings; meals/snacks available.

Right *The characteristic charm of rural Tuscany.*
Far right *A flower-bedecked stairway leads to a village house in the commune of Barberino.*

The village of Barberino, officially Barberino Val d'Elsa, lies outside Chianti Classico but its commune stretches well inside and includes several major estates. It is easily reached from Panzano or Castellina and is a short distance from the San Donato exit of the Florence–Siena *superstrada*.

Arriving from Panzano turn right (or from Castellina, left) at the junction for San Donato. You pass through La Piazza, so tiny it has little to offer beyond an espresso. A couple of kilometres further on Le Filigare, off to the left, is the first Barberino estate. At the next junction take the left fork (signposted Castellina) for Barberino's heartland. The right fork leads into San Donato in Poggio, a sub-commune of Barberino, with an impressive 11th-century church. The hills are fairly steep and territory mixed: vines, plenty of olive grove and pine forest. Many vineyards have galestro soil, a tough clay-slate, excellent for quality wine.

The first track to the right leads to Villa Francesca; the second, to Casa Sola, a large *agriturismo* complex about three kilometres further down. After these junctions you pass Casa Emma and Fattoria La Ripa. Then turn right towards Olena. From there continue straight along the narrow unmade road to Isole e Olena, Castello della Paneretta and Fattoria Monsanto respectively. These last two are castles in the true sense of the word: four-square, solid-built, strongly defensive structures. The rivalry between Florence and Siena today amounts to no more than a friendly joke. In centuries past it led to years of serious warfare and fortified castles were a necessary protection against invasion.

CASTELLINA

RECOMMENDED PRODUCERS

Casanova di Pietrafitta
Tel: 0577 740200
Attractive farmhouse reconstructed in traditional form. Tiny estate. *Agriturismo*; tastings for small groups.

Poggio al Sorbo
Tel: 0577 733518
Very pretty, small 12th-century estate. Good wines. Also produce oil, olive pâté and preserves. *Agriturismo* with swimming pool.

Ruffino
Tel: 055 8368307
Enormous company based at Pontassieve in Chianti Rufina producing large quantities of generic Chianti and basic Chianti Classico. Also has a number of properties in central Tuscany – Santedame, here in Castellina for example – for higher quality output. Huge range includes Chianti Classico Riserva Ducale; super-tuscans Cabreo Il Borgo (red), Cabreo La Pietra (white); Libaio (Chardonnay/Sauvignon), Nero del Tondo (Pinot Nero) and many others. Also has estates in Montalcino and Montepulciano.

Buondonno
Tel: 0577 733603
Small family-run estate. *Agriturismo*.

Nittardi
Tel: 0577 740269
Situated between Florence and Siena in an area whose ownership was once hotly disputed, this was first documented as a massive fortress called Nectar Dei. At one time run by Michelangelo's nephew. 120ha of woodland but just eight hectares of vineyard. Wines (predominantly Chianti Classico) are stylish and high quality. *Agriturismo*. Meals, snacks and tastings on request.

Il Villino
Tel: 0577 741178
19th-century farmhouse with *agriturismo*.

Tregole
Tel: 0577 740991
Improving wines, *agriturismo*.

* **Castello di Fonterutoli**
Tel: 0577 740309
Run by the Mazzei family since 1435. 34ha of vineyard; highly regarded wines. Chianti Classico Ser Lapo, super-tuscan Concerto (Sangiovese/Cabernet) top the list.

San Leonino
Tel: 0290 960931
Bought in 1988 and completely restructured by Velm SpA, a Milanese company with properties also in

* Castellina

If Chianti Classico is the heart of Chianti then Castellina, luxuriating in the full title Castellina in Chianti, is the heart of the heart. The commune has more open country-side than Greve or Barberino; the enchanting scenery is softer, with the occasional grassy field and the vine-covered hills come in beautiful flowing sweeps. Vines grow mainly on alberese or sandstone but there are outcrops of clay, quite heavy in parts. There are also some magnificent rows of cypress trees lined up like tin soldiers. The trees usually appear in pairs, either many at a time lining driveways to important properties, or individually: two cypresses traditionally mark land ownership boundaries.

Castellina is a 15–20 minute drive along the Chiantigiana from Panzano, it takes the same time from the San Donato exit of the Florence–Siena *superstrada*. It is also reasonably close to Poggibonsi and San Gimignano (see p74), to Radda (see p58) and not far from Siena. Castellina is the perfect centre where you can eat well, drink well and find plenty of pleasant places to stay overnight.

The town has a quiet, confident air, busy without bustle. The central piazza is tiny, but the streets running off it mix shops, businesses and houses with calm ease. Castellina is built on a ridge over 550 metres high. Behind the main

Main picture *Dawn mist envelopes a Chianti farmhouse and vineyard.* Below *Fresh ravioli, made with a variety of stuffings.*

Montalcino and Montepulciano. Now high-tech. *Agritursimo.* Group tastings.

Fortezza di Tuopina
Tel: 0577 743073
Large estate, also produces olive oil.

Lilliano
Tel: 0577 743070
Large estate owned by the Principi Ruspoli. Medieval in layout but has been successively restructured. Well sited vineyards. *Agriturismo.*

Rodano
Tel: 0577 743107
Elegant wines made from the best of over 100ha of vineyard.

San Fabiano Calcinaia
Tel: 0577 979232
Traces remain of an ancient medieval site here. A fairly large estate with vineyards on two sites at San Fabiano and Cellole. Balanced and long-lived wines. *Agriturismo.* Light meals.

street is the long covered corridor of Via delle Volte. On one side are the backs of buildings, the other side looks over Chianti and the view is breathtaking.

It is worth tracing two routes from the town: Castellina north, and Castellina south and southwest (this latter is known as Castellina Scalo). If you have followed the Panzano and Barberino routes and arrived from San Donato/Barberino you will have covered some of Castellina north already. Try retracing the route from the other direction, if you can, to see how different the countryside looks.

The north route leads out of Castellina on the Chiantigiana past Casanova di Pietrafitta on the left, then Il Faggeto and Quercetorta (both left) and Pietrafitta on the right. A forested, vine-free stretch leads to the San Donato junction. Take this left fork and after La Piazza you can take either the 'main route' or the 'short cut'. The former takes you past Poggio al Sorbo and slices through part of Barberino. Follow signs to Castellina to emerge back in Castellina at a turn-off to Ruffino's Santedame estate and a minute later, a layby (right). For the 'short cut', after La Piazza turn left (to Nittardi). Only half the distance of the alternative, but one of Chianti's famous 'white roads' (unmade, narrow and bumpy) so it can takes twice as long to cover but could be twice as much fun. It passes Buondonno and after a short while, a side road to Nittardi, then it meanders through the countryside emerging at the

Rocca delle Macie
Tel 0577 743220
Large complex in a tiny 14th-century village. Almost 250 hectares of vines. Large quantities of good-value, everyday Chianti Classico and about a dozen other wines as well as top Chianti Classico Fizzano and super-Tuscan Ser Gioveto (Sangiovese). Olive oil and honey also produced. Very hospitable (be sure to book). Direct sales and tastings. *Agriturismo.*

Castellare
Tel: 0577 740362
Split off from a larger property in the 1960s. Now has 20 hectares of well aspected vineyard. Rather stark cellars. Fine Chianti Classico, super-Tuscan I Sodi di San Niccolò (Sangiovese/Malvasia Nera). Also Chardonnay, Sauvignon and Vin Santo. Olive oil. *Agriturismo.*

HOTELS

Tenuta di Ricavo
Ricavo *Tel: 0577 740221*
High-quality hotel.
Salivolpi
Castellina *Tel: 0577 740484*
Traditionally structured and furnished, simple, restful and pleasant. Open in winter.
Hotel San Leonino
San Leonino
In similar style but slightly more up-market than Salivolpi.
Casafrassi
Quercegrossa *Tel: 0577 740621*
Well reputed.

Main picture (top) *Canaiolo is an official constituent of the Chianti blend, but is being used progressively less as, according to current thinking, the more Sangiovese in the blend, the finer the wine.*
Above *Cypress trees form a dramatic boundary across the top of a Tuscan hill.*

lay-by mentioned above. The view over western Chianti at this point is magnificent: San Gimignano is distinctly visible if the weather is clear. Head back into Castellina over the Macia Morta, a 600 metre-high ridge.

For the southern route, leave Castellina on the Chiantigiana towards Siena. Passing Il Villino and Tregoleare to the left, five minutes more brings you to the peaceful hamlet of Fonterutoli, much of it connected with winemaking for the Castello di Fonterutoli estate and most of it owned by the estate's noble Mazzei family. The road then skims the corner of the commune of Castelnuovo Berardenga (see p66). Take a sharp right at the next

RESTAURANTS

Albergaccio di Castellina
Tel: 0577 741042
Well known and reputed *trattoria* with much emphasis on its wine list. Well flavoured food, traditional Tuscan with modern touches. Not cheap but good value. Closed Sundays.

La Torre
Tel 0577 740236
Nearly always open, always busy; the essence of a good *trattoria*. Ample portions of simple, traditional dishes, well cooked and flavoursome. Hopeless for weight-watchers. Fairly good range of Chianti and one or two other wines. Closed Fridays.

Pietrafitta
Località Pietrafitta *Tel 0577 741153*
For a real break from Tuscan traditions — dishes from all over the world, unsurprisingly as proprietors are New Zealanders. Wine list international too. Always open.

ENOTECA

Enoteca le Cantuccio
Via Ferruccio 25

Bottega del Vino Chianti Classico
Via della Rocca 10.

junction onto an unmade road, past Le Galozzole (which sells direct) to San Leonino. As you approach, Fortezza di Tuopina is on the left. This is a particularly pretty part of the commune: open, soft and with panoramic views. One of Tuscany's most majestic rows of cypress trees can soon be seen. A little further on the impressive Lilliano site practically blocks the road. Scoot round behind it and head west (towards Poggibonsi), another section with wonderful views. You pass the castle of Bibbiano on the left and rise rapidly to Rodano then descend to San Fabiano Calcinaia. The estate buildings are situated just outside the Chianti Classico border, so turn back and at Lilliano head left over a narrow rutted road towards Rocca delle Macie, one of Chianti's largest estates. From there you can amble back to Castellina at your leisure.

Above *A farmhouse near Castellina in Chianti. Vines in this part of Chianti grow on* alberese *or sandstone but there are outcrops of clay in parts.*

For another fix of the countryside, you could make a third trip. Turn sharp left just through Castellina, passing Cellole to see Castellare, Rufone, Brancaia, Villa Rosa, Picini and Gretole. From there you could continue to Poggibonsi and San Gimignano – or just take a look around.

Radda

RADDA

RECOMMENDED PRODUCERS

Aiola
Tel: 0577 322615
Originally a 12th-century fortified castle, Aiola is famous for its resistance on the Siena front line in 1554. Now a welcoming mid-sized estate with a pretty villa and large tasting area. super-tuscan Logaiolo (Sangiovese), Bianco Val d'Arbia is produced as is Chianti Classico.

Terrabianca
Tel: 0577 738544
A 17th-century farmhouse, completely modernised, with its own wine shop.

Poddere Terreno
Tel: 0577 738312
15th-century farmhouse. Soft, all-too-drinkable wines. Welcoming, cheery owners. *Agriturismo.*

The commune of Radda in eastern Chianti is one of Chianti Classico's highest, with some estates at an altitude of over 600 metres. There are some pretty steep slopes and roads often follow hill ridges. The woodland has more deciduous trees than further west, and there are even a few areas of scrub. The soil is darker, red-tinged in parts, although *alberese* dominates south of the town and sandstone in the higher areas to the north.

Radda town is a disappointment. It is marred by an unsightly brick depot at its southern end and, although its centre is quite pretty, it lacks the personality of Castellina or Panzano. It is, though, where the Consorzio Chianti Classico (see p45) was founded in 1924: the spot where their offices were sited (by the Relais Vignale) is marked by a plaque.

Radda is best reached from Castellina. There is a fairly direct route (10–15 minutes) eastward, but it has no particular wine interest. The longer route, a glorious twisting and heavily wooded road, is a much more attractive alternative. Head out southward from Castellina on the Chiantigiana and branch left after five minutes onto an unmade road signposted Vagliagli. A few old granite wheels, once used for crushing olives, lie along the roadside and the hamlet of Fonterutoli is on the right. There is also a signpost right to

Below *Vagliagli is small, tranquil and very pretty, an ideal spot for a gentle stroll.*

Above left *The name* Pizzicheria *is special to Florence and its environs but most small towns have at least one shop selling cheeses and* salumi *with other foodstuffs.*
Above *Radda's vineyards tend to be on steep slopes. Buildings are on hill tops - a legacy of its war-torn past.*

'necropoli etrusca' but unless you have a four-wheel drive vehicle it is better to reach this small Etruscan burial ground on foot. The next estate up on the left is Tregole. The road snakes up and down, then onto a ridge with better views. Quercegrossa is visible down in the valley to the right.

At the entrance to Vagliagli, before turning left to go through the village, take a detour down the slope and right, then left after about 100 metres. This leads to a wonderfully peaceful, forested lane, a 'protection oasis' (protected from hunting) and eventually to Dievole, a large, modernistic wine estate. Vagliagli itself is a small, pretty hill-top village and despite the horrors of trying to pronounce its name, is well worth visiting if only for a breath of air and a bite to eat.

Head back north towards Radda, first passing Aiola then Terrabianca before an estate-free saunter into the town. From Radda a couple of return trips can be made which are easily completed in half a day. The route not be missed is a round trip. At the first crossroads through the town turn left, then right a couple of kilometres further along. The next fork is the beginning (and end) of your circle. Fork right and you rise through the typical Chianti combination of vineyard, olive grove and wood to Podere Terreno (right) and Pruneto (along a lane to the left) then, a few minutes further, Volpaia. The church on the left is Santa Maria Novella; you will pass it on your return.

The cluster of buildings that makes up Castello di Volpaia is almost a village in its own right. Apart from cellars, winemaking areas and a *frantoio,* there are workmen's houses, a church, even a small general store and bar – the coffee is excellent. (Park carefully if you stop here because there are often consignments of wine being moved about.) Back on the road, after a couple of large bends to the left, turn left at the T-junction and head back down, passing Castelvecchi and the Santa Maria Novella church. The beautifully preserved, serene Volpaia is now across the valley.

Once back down at the T-junction, turn left towards Radda but at the next junction go left again (instead of right

Pruneto
Tel: 0577 738532
Small, welcoming family-run estate (in spite of the fierce guard dog). Just one *agriturismo* apartment. The wines are excellent: must book tastings.

✽ **Castello di Volpaia**
Tel: 0577 738066
One of Chianti's highest (500m) and most highly regarded estates producing powerful, assertive, rich wines. Produces super-Tuscans Coltassala (mainly Sangiovese) and Balifico (mainly Cabernet and Sangiovese), Torniello (white, Sauvignon-Sémillon), Bianco Val d'Arbia, Vin Santo as well as Chianti Classico from 37ha. Tuscany's only legally authorised producer of wine vinegar. Also makes olive oil and honey. Direct sales. *Agriturismo.*

Castelvecchi
Tel: 0577 738050
The site was an important medieval settlement and an Etruscan and Roman communications point. Named Castelvecchi in the 18th century when owned by the de'Vecchi family. *Agriturismo.*

to head back to the town). On this road there is no shortage of vines or estates. Huge swathes of vineyard appear on your left. A lane a couple of minutes further along on the left leads up steeply to Monte Vertine, an estate which is situated high on a ridge, with the most glorious of views over the Chianti hills. Just past the Monte Vertine cut-off is the Poggerino estate (on the right).

The next track to the left leads up to the hill-top Podere Capaccia, just across the Pesa River Valley from Volpaia, with views as good as those of Monte Vertine. The property centres around a remarkably well preserved medieval hamlet, but beware, the road is poor and steep, hard work for a small car and extremely hard work if the road is wet. Forking off the track is Crognole.

The next estate, another few minutes further along, is Castello d'Albola, then come two fat towers in the centre of a mass of *poderi* (small farms or plots), each with its own small farmhouse. This tended to be the pattern of most estates during the *mezzadria* (see p9) but now each *podere* and accompanying house are owned outright. Albola itself, out of sight of those daunting towers, is a glorious, quiet little place and has harmoniously restored estate buildings. It is also Radda's northernmost estate, so it is time to turn back and head towards Gaiole.

Fattoria di Monte Vertine
Tel: 0577 738009
One of the few estates not belonging to either Chianti Classico Consorzio and thus producing only super-Tuscans. Owned by the jovial Sergio Manetti, who left a businessman's life to become a wine producer and never looked back. The wines are terrific and still improving each year: Monte Vertine (a Chianti Classico equivalent), Le Pergole Torte (100% Sangiovese), Il Sodaccio (mainly Sangiovese), M (the obscurely named white), Vin Santo and others.

Poggerino
Tel: 0577 738232
Small, friendly estate, 13th-century origins. Good, attractive, well fruited wines. *Agriturismo.*

Podere Capaccia
Tel: 0577 738385
Small estate, with high-quality wines. Chianti Classico and super-Tuscan Querciagrande (Sangiovese). *Agriturismo*, meals or snacks can be provided.

Crognole
Tel: 0577 738368
The house was a watch-tower in the 13th century.

HOTELS

Relais Fattoria Vignale
Radda Tel 0577 738300
Calm, peaceful rooms, traditionally designed and furnished but with all modern conveniences. Swimming pool.

RESTAURANTS

La Taverna del Chianti
Via del Sergente, Vagliagli
Tel: 0577 322532
Simple *trattoria*: very good food.
Closed in winter.

Ristorante Vignale
Radda *Tel: 0577 738094*
Elegant, traditional dishes with class and refinement, but costly.

Le Vigne
Radda *Tel: 0577 738640*
A rare chance to dine right in the middle of a vineyard.

FOOD SHOPPING/ENOTECHE

Enoteche/Paninoteca
Radda
Combined wine and bread shop – inspired thinking.

Castello di Vagliagli
Vagliagli
Adjacent to restaurant.

Porciatti
Radda, Piazza IV Novembre 1
Wide range of high quality foodstuffs.

Left *The stone façades of buildings in Radda have a soft, warm glow.*
Top *Spring is the season of delicate* zucchini *(courgette) flowers, broad beans, sometimes eaten raw in salads, and asparagus.*

Above *The hill top town of Radda can be seen in the background, overlooking the convent of Santa Maria. Radda has some beautifully preserved old buildings which include several wine estates.*

Gaiole

Gaiole is only five kilometres southeast of Radda, but even the most direct road is two to three times as long. Some estates are as close to Radda as to Gaiole, so the best starting point is Radda. The tour can be completed in half a day.

Leave Radda the way you came in, but at the junction for Vagliagli and Lecchi, go towards Lecchi instead of Vagliagli. Almost immediately fork right up to a pretty, tranquil church, San Giusto in Salcio. You get good views of Radda from its terrace, which is ideal for a quick sandwich.

Moving south into Gaiole territory the terrain becomes quite mixed. The soil is practically all *alberese* in this western part (sandstone in the east) and vineyards abound. There is a gradual increase in the amount of olive cultivation. A long track on the right leads to the impressive San Polo in Rosso and another, almost immediately after, rises along a curved ridge to Castello di Ama. Follow the signs for 'Fattoria di Ama', not just 'Ama' or 'Casanuova di Ama', which is a separate estate. Castello di Ama is large and functional but blends well into the countryside. Even if you do not plan to stop, it is worth driving right round the complex for the unbroken panorama of the countryside.

Just before Lecchi, a delightful little place, there is an almost perfectly conical hill to the left, and nestling within

GAIOLE

RECOMMENDED PRODUCERS

Castello di San Polo
Tel: 0577 746045
Imposing castle, completely restructured, with small church containing many frescoes. The estate now produces refined Chianti Classico, super-tuscans Cetinaia (100% Sangiovese) Coccole (Sauvignon/Sémillon) and others from well-sited vineyard.

Castello di Ama
Tel: 0577 746031
Large estate, high-quality, stylish wines. Chianti Classico mainly from single vineyards. Also an unusually large array of other grape varieties: Sauvignon, Pinot Grigio, Chardonnay, Merlot and Pinot Nero, produced as single varietals from separate vineyards.

Podere il Palazzino
Tel: 0577 747008
Best known for super-Tuscan Grosso Senese (100% Sangiovese). Must book for tasting sessions.

Castello di Cacchiano
Tel: 0577 747018
Owned by the Ricasoli Firidolfi family since medieval times. *Agriturismo.*

Brolio
Tel: 0577 749066
Gaiole's most magnificent castle. Huge production from good sites, once well reputed but, following ownership and shareholding changes, the wines, labelled Brolio and Barone Ricasoli, have been variable.

Rocca di Castagnoli
Tel: 0577 731004
Large property. Chianti Classicos Poggio a'Frati and Capraia. Also super-tuscans Stielle (Cabernet Sauvignon/Sangiovese), Mont'Ornello (100% Cabernet Sauvignon), Molino delle Balze (Chardonnay) and others. All highly rated wines.

Rietine
Tel: 0577 731110
The village is also well worth a look as, unusually, it was planned on a circular system around the church. *Agriturismo.*

Giorgio Regni
Tel: 0577 731005
Named after the former proprietor, the estate is now becoming known as **Fattoria Valtellina** after a herd of Valtelline cattle (from Lombardy) which were once raised here. Good wines, fairly priced. *Agriturismo.*

Above Bruschetta al pomodoro, *a local speciality – bread topped with a tomato sauce.*

Two views of the large estate Rocca di Castagnoli: the cellars (left) *and* (below) *the* rocca *(fortress) itself.*

it is the village of Monteluco. Past Lecchi towards San Sano, it gets flatter and wilder and Mediterranean pines start to appear. A few minutes past San Sano, another pretty, well-served village, the road curves left dramatically, then stops abruptly at a T-junction. To go straight into Gaiole, go left, but the tour continues to the right, into wild-looking terrain. Turn left to Monti at the next set of signposts and you join the Strada dei Castelli del Chianti. This part of the commune was on the front line in the Florence – Siena wars. The many high-points, with wide views, were perfect for defence. Gaiole *castelli* are castles indeed and well fortified.

Castello di Meleto
Tel: 0577 749496
190ha around the heavily-set 12th-century fortressed castle. Once owned by the Ricasoli family.

Castello di San Donato in Perano
Tel: 0577 733533
This estate is more interesting for its history than its wines. The site was first documented as long ago as the 10th century. In the 16th the owners, the Strozzi family from Florence, consolidated all the various holdings and by the end of the century it had become a smart villa at the centre of a hamlet.

Badia a Coltibuono
Tel: 0577 749498
A monastery for over 700 years and now owned by the Stucchi Prinetti family. The wines, from 60ha of mature vines mostly at Monti, are often remarkably long-lived and among the top Chiantis. In addition to Chianti Classico, super-Tuscan Sangioveto (100% Sangiovese); Vin Santo; Coltibuono Rosso, Rosato and Bianco. Also a shop selling produce from the estate. Own restaurant (see below). The estate also has a well known cookery school. Church services are still held regularly in the chapel.

Riecine
Tel: 0577 749527
Small estate owned by Englishman John Dunkley and producing fine, intense, elegant wines. Excellent Chianti Classico, also super-Tuscan La Gioia (Sangiovese). Must book for tastings.

Villa Vistarenni
Tel: 0577 738476
200ha estate with 35ha under vines. Chianti Classico Assolo and Villa Vistarenni; super-Tuscan Codirosso; Vin Santo and Bianco Val D'Arbia. These are very much wines to watch. *Agriturismo.*

HOTEL

Hotel San Sano
San Sano *Tel 0577 746130*
Comfortable hotel with well appointed rooms. Swimming pool. Own wines and other produce.

RESTAURANTS

Ristorante Carloni
Via G Pucini 24, Gaiole
Tel: 0577 749549
Inauspicious entrance but well signposted in a side-street just outside the town. Simple Tuscan fare prepared from good, well cooked ingredients. Fair local wine selection. Not expensive. Closed Wednesdays.

La Grotta della Rana
San Sano *Tel: 0577 746020*
Good, traditional food; seats outside in summer.

Just past Monti is an important Chianti Classico 2000 experimental plot (see p45). At the next T-junction turn right (left takes you to Podere Il Palazzino). Almost immediately to the left is the lane to Castello di Cacchiano's cypress-lined driveway, steep, but with fantastic views.

The imposing Castello di Brolio soon appears up ahead. The original Chianti 'recipe' was laid down here almost two centuries ago by the owner, Barone Bettino Ricasoli. The cellars and winemaking plant are easily visible from the road. Turn left at the next junction, then right at the next, branching off the Gaiole road onto a 'white road'. After a short while Rietine appears to the left and then the 11th-century Rocca di Castagnoli ahead. Take the next left and four estates follow in quick succession. Rocca di Castagnoli is immediately on the right, followed by Rietine on the left. Giorgio Regni appears next on the left. A little further on at the end of a cypress-lined driveway is the Castello di Meleto, another important defence in the Florence – Siena wars. Follow the road down. The buildings you pass are Meleto's cellars. Turn right at the T-junction to reach, finally, Gaiole town.

There is another cluster of estates north of the town. If time is short, go straight through Gaiole (direction Montevarchi), heading for the first major three-way junction (about five kilmetres). Otherwise, for the scenic route,

Far left *Some of Gaiole's castles are just as imposing inside as out. This is in Brolio.*
Above *The clear light of a crisp winter day highlights the outlines of the villa of Badia a Coltibuono.*
Left *Castello di Brolio – as classic a castle as any in Chianti.*
Below *Necks of Chianti Classico carry a DOCG approved sticker.*

leave Gaiole westward (left) partially through the town on an unmade road towards Spaltenna. Shortly before the end of this cut-through, with its extraordinary views from sandstone ridges, is Castello di San Donato in Perano.

Turn right at the end (towards Montevarchi), heading up to the three-way junction you could have reached directly from Gaiole. The left turn is to the leading estate of Badia a Coltibuono, 630metres high and unmissable; the right turn (towards Gaiole) leads you to Tiorcia and Riecine. For Riecine take the first lane to the left, then first right.

This almost completes Gaiole, so go back along the ridge towards Radda. Eventually the view opens out and you come to a junction. You are practically back at Radda but before heading right into town, turn left for Gaiole's (perhaps Chianti Classico's) most august view: the château (no other word quite describes it) of Vistarenni perched up in the hills at the end of a long, cypress-lined driveway leading from the road (it takes a good four minutes to drive along it). Majesty indeed.

L'Osteria di Badia a Coltibuono
Coltibuono *Tel: 0577 749424*
Simple cooking: *crostini, salumi*, home-made pasta, plainly cooked meats; all with plenty of flavour. Wines from the estate. Closed Mondays.

Castelnuovo Berardenga

Castelnuovo Berardenga is Chianti Classico's southernmost commune. The countryside is not dissimilar to southern Gaiole with its open, sometimes wild, sometimes restful views, but there is a warmer feel to the surroundings and the olive is in greater evidence. Soils are quite mixed.

It is not difficult to reach from Gaiole, although it can take over half an hour, but for the most convenient tour of its estates it is best to start from Siena or Castellina. This tour assumes Siena is the start-point: if you are coming from Castellina you will need to read backwards. The roads are quite fast, so half a day is ample time to allow.

From Siena (or the Florence–Siena *superstrada:* Castelnuovo is about an hour from Florence) heading towards Arezzo, fork left at the Asciano turn-off, go through Montaperti and into Chianti Classico. Looking behind,

CASTELNUOVO BERARDENGA

RECOMMENDED PRODUCERS

San Felice
Tel: 0577 359087
Some of the 190ha are used for research into clones of local varieties, others are experimental for the Chianti Classico 2000 project. Fine wines: Chianti Classico Poggio Rosso, Villa La Pagliaia, Il Grigio and Campo del Civettino; super-Tuscan Vigorello (Sangiovese); Vin Santo; Bianco Val d'Arbia; Chardonnay. Olive oil.

Villa a Sesta
Tel: 0577 359014. Agriturismo.

San Cosma
Tel: 0577 359084
Small estate run by a Dane, Bent Myhre. Unusually styled but good wines. Direct sales. *Agriturismo.*

Villa Arceno
Tel: 0577 359066
Wines undergoing great developments. Also oil.

Felsina
Also known as **Berardenga Felsina, Felsina Berardenga** and **Fattoria di Felsina**.
Tel: 0577 355117
Giuseppe Mazzocolin, intelligent, studious but with a delicious sense of humour and his friend, gifted consultant Franco Bernabei, are making wines to die for. Refined, powerful, complex and characterful, these are the pace-setters. Chianti Classico and cru Vigneto Rancia, super-tuscan Fontalloro (100% Sangiovese), I Sistri (Chardonnay), Maestro Raro (Cabernet) and others are all excellent. Top-class oil too.

Left *The pretty village of Villa A Sesta, seemingly unchanged for centuries.*
Bottom left and far left *In Borgo San Felice, everything is designed to be restful and pleasing to the eye.*

you'll catch magical views of the Siena towers in the distance. At the first major junction turn right towards San Felice to tour eastern Castelnuovo. Bossi appears on the right after a couple of minutes, swiftly followed by San Felice, which is a joy. Although dominated by the estate it is a perfectly cared-for *borgo* (hamlet) with its own piazza, church and *frantoio*. Past San Felice turn right at the next junction (if coming from Gaiole you join here) and proceed to Villa a Sesta.

Just before the next junction, a hub for two short visits, San Cosma is on the right. At the junction, turn left to San Gusmé, a fairly ordinary village, then right to Villa Arceno. This is a huge and magnificent property, one of very few which was not broken up, and remains completely unchanged by the passing of the *mezzadria* (see p9). Its workers' houses are scattered widely around the august villa and its cellars, stables and granary. These houses are now being converted to *agriturismo*. There is also a hotel on site and more houses are being built for sale.

Back at the 'hub' junction take the road ahead, south towards Castelnuovo Berardenga town. A little over three kilometres down is Felsina, right on the Chianti Classico border but producing some of the zone's best wines.

At the 'hub' once more, take a sharp left (southwest). Just a few minutes brings you to a hefty gateway on the left with a long drive: the approach to Pagliarese, whose neighbour is Castell'in Villa. The comparative warmth of the area is demonstrated by the thriving Mediterranean pines.

Before long, you arrive back where the tour started. This time carry on westward, to Pianella and the Arbia river, the bisection point of Castelnuovo. On maps the Arbia is prefixed 'T' for *torrente* rather than 'F' for *fiume* (river). It looks nothing like a torrent, however, it is just a dribble. The 'T' warns that, when in spate, it can become a torrent indeed, as the smashed bridge over the Arbia frighteningly displays.

Bossi
Tel: 0577 359048
For *agriturismo*.

Pagliarese
Tel: 0577 359070
Originally a 13th-century Sienese fort defending against Florentine attack, now a middle-sized quality-conscious estate. super-Tuscan Camerlengo, Bianco Val d'Arbia, Vin Santo and others are made as well as Chianti Classico. Olive oil. Direct sales. *Agriturismo*, with swimming pool.

Castell'in Villa
Tel: 0577 359074
Owned by Greek Princess Pignatelli della Leonessa, this largish estate produces consistently good wines. Heavy concentration on Chianti Classico, but other wines also made.

Castello di Ceretto
Tel: 0577 356996
Often known by the name of its owner, fashion designer **Emilio Pucci**.

Castello di Selvole
Tel: 0577 322662
17 out of over 160ha along a well exposed hill ridge at 450m are under vine. Major *agriturismo* enterprise, swimming pool, tennis and volley ball courts as well as mountain bike hire. Olive oil. Direct sales.

Poggio dell'Oliviera
Tel: 0577 322652
Good wines made on this tiny (3ha) estate.

Fattoria Corsignano
Tel: 0577 322610
Agriturismo.

Valiano
Tel: 0577 356850
Traces of Etruscan settlements dot the 225ha property. Extensive olive groves. Direct sales.

Fattoria Il Castagno
Tel: 0577 50459
Some parts of building are 10th century. *Agriturismo*.

Podere Olmo
Tel: 0577 327297
Well sited vineyards. *Agriturismo*.

HOTELS

Borgo San Felice Hotel
San Felice
Tel: 0577 359260
Part of Châteaux and Relais group. Swimming pool, tennis courts. Part of the San Felice hamlet and designed to blend in with it. Luxurious, smart but comfortable and characterful. Also a (costly) restaurant.

Villa Arceno
Tel: 0577 357292
A Relais hotel.
Also a (costly) restaurant.

Villa Gloria
Quercegrossa
Good quality hotel.

Fine estates are less concentrated in western Castelnuovo but the scenery is possibly even better. Almost immediately on the left is a cypress-lined driveway to Vitignano and, butting out into the road, Macia. A few minutes' further up there is a signpost to the *ruderi* (ruins) of the Castello di Ceretto. Little remains now of the ruins and they are not easy to find.

The next estate on the right is Monteropoli. Continue past the small church of Asciata then, as the road bends left,

Above *Only a few wine producers in Tuscany make grappa; Vin Santo is the traditional post-prandial drink.*
Above right *Vines in Castelnuovo Berardenga, Chianti Classico's southernmost commune, benefit from the comparative warmth of the area.*

Castello di Selvole is up on the right. This big complex also centres on a beautiful villa. Its approach is attractively lined by olive plants instead of the usual cypresses.

At the next cluster of road signs you can take a quick detour left to see Borgo Scopeto, although sometimes the entrance is closed and you cannot see more than part of a villa behind a mass of olives. Otherwise head onward (you are quite close to Vagliagli here) before taking a sharp V-shaped turn down to the left. Immediately on your right is Poggio dell'Oliviera. In the next few minutes you pass near Vigna a Sole, Fattoria Corsignano and then Valiano, another important property. The Certosa di Pontignano is across to the left. Approaching Valiano, a mysterious, avenue of cypress trees appears and looking back, it is clear that the road's construction interrupted their path. The road curves to the right, Fattoria Il Castagno appears a minute later on the left, and soon after you meet the Siena–Castellina road.

Turn right and you soon pass Podere Olmo; the last curves of Castelnuovo Berardenga are behind you. You are now at Quercegrossa (in the Castellina tour). The unmarked commune boundary is a few kilometres along the road.

RESTAURANTS

La Bottega del Trenta
Villa a Sesta
Tel: 0577 359226
Unusual. In an old house with old furnishings, few tables, friendly service. Innovative dishes from local ingredients. Extraordinarily good value, especially for local wines. Tables in the courtyard in summer. Good value. Closed winter.

Il Molino delle Bagnaie
Loc Le Bagnaie (Pianella)
Tel: 0577 47062
In an old mill on the River Arbia. Typical local *trattoria*, wholesome food. Good selection of Chianti.

Castelnuovo Berardenga (left and above) *lies just outside the Chianti Classico zone but is bigger than other similar commune centres and has an unassuming and friendly atmosphere.*

Siena

SIENA

ENOTECHE

Enoteca San Domenico
Viadel Paradiso 56
Good wine selection, mainly Tuscan, but also other Italian and some French; grappa, acquevite and other spirits, interesting snacks, pastries and small cakes. Sales only, unfortunately: no tastings.

Enoteca le Bollicine
Via Giovanni Dupré 64
Same owner as San Domenico. Here you can taste and drink good wines. Plates of cheese and *salumi* available.

Azienda Consorzio Provinciale Siena
Via Pianigiani
Wines and foods from the province.

Siena is a significant staging post on any wine tour of Tuscany not just for its own delights but for its proximity to most of the major wine areas. Chianti Classico's more southern communes, San Gimignano, Montepulciano and Montalcino, can all be reached within an hour's drive and it is a good start-off point for many of the region's important non-wine towns and villages too.

The city is inextricably linked with the *Palio* (see page 73), but also proudly displays its foods, wines, culture and historical warrior prowess from its commanding hill top position.

Arriving at Siena from any direction is a memorable experience as its famous twin towers hive into view, sometimes from a great distance, at other times, not until you are within a couple of minutes of the outskirts. Reaching the centre is also memorable, but for other reasons. Siena's roads weave back and forth in elegant but disorientating curves across the hills. There are car parks around the compact centre's edges and a good bus system if you park further afield.

Inside the practically traffic-free centre, cobbled streets twist and arch around the slopes. The main streets are crowded during the *passeggiata* (evening stroll), but when dinner-time arrives they empty within minutes. In winter

Below *The Campo, lying just outside the original city walls, is where carriages and carts were unloaded and their wares taken to market.*

the city can then take on the aspect of a ghost town, the narrow streets dark and shuttered – making arrival at the Campo or the Duomo eerily exciting. In summer there is much more life. Even so, it is quieter after dark than one would expect, with folk making merry in *trattorie* and restaurants rather than on the streets.

Siena is divided into 17 *contrade* (very roughly tiny boroughs), each of which has its own shield, colours and flag. Rivalry between the *contrade* is intense and reaches unbelievable levels during the *Palio*. A good selection of plates and plaques and so on, decorated with the colours of each *contrada*, are available to buy.

ENOTECA ITALIANA

Also known as the Enoteca Permanente, the Enoteca Nazionale, the Enoteca di Siena and La Fortezza, the Enoteca is a vast collection of hundreds of wines from all over Italy, beautifully presented in a vaulted cellar actually within the old Medici fortress. It is not a complete collection, though. Producers choose to have their wines displayed, on payment of an annual fee, as long as a tasting committee is satisfied. Naturally, it is strongest in Tuscan wines. The wines are also on sale. Above the cellar is a spacious area for tasting or drinking and there are tables outside during the summer months.

Every day three wines are suggested for tasting but any wine on display is available for about 2,000 lire per glass. Crackers or perhaps a nibble of cheese are available – classic tasting accompaniments. Open every day: from midday until

Above *Rehearsal for the* Palio. *If lucky, you may see flag-tossing in the Campo. Even better, street dinners are held and visitors can buy tickets. Ask at the tourist office.*

HOTELS

As a major tourist centre, Siena has a wide range of hotels. None, though, has particular wine links.

RESTAURANTS

Le Logge
Via del Porrione 33 *Tel: 0577 48013*
Generous portions of traditional Tuscan dishes but with a light touch. Good selection of mainly Tuscan wines but try proprietor's wine from their property in Montalcino. Excellent value.

Mariotti da Mugolone
Via dei Pellegrini 8 *Tel: 0577 282235*
More traditional than this it is hard to come by. A few special bottles. Not cheap though.

Il Giuggiolo
Via Massetana 30 *Tel: 0577 274295*
Good, traditional, local dishes. But go for the wines which are given the most care and interest in Siena.

Da Enzo
Via Camollia 49 Tel: 0577 281277
A rare chance to eat fish, fresh daily, though it can be costly. Good, eclectic wine list, not restricted to local wines.

Above *Siena's elegantly curved streets are steeply sloping or stepped.*
Left *Siena's famous* panforte: *a spicy mix of candied fruit and nuts.*
Right *The Duomo dominates Siena's skyline.*
Far right *Siena is wonderful for shopping, notably for food and wine.*

12.30am in the winter and to 1.00am in the summer. (Tel: 0577 288497.) The Fortezza is well signposted but street lighting sometimes fails. Take a torch.

Il Biondo
Via del Rustichetto 10
Tel: 0577 280739
Centrally located; more than decent, traditional, local dishes; small but interesting wine list. Fairly priced.

Castelvecchio
Via Castelvecchio 65 *Tel: 0577 49586*
Former stables in the oldest part of town, carefully refurbished. Range of dishes but with emphasis on local flavours and organic ingredients. Tuscan wines plus non-Tuscan Italians.

Il Ghibellino
Via dei Pellegrini 26 *Tel: 0577 288079*
Simple, excellently flavoured food relying on good ingredients. Short but well balanced wine list.

FOOD SHOPPING

Siena has many speciality food shops. Even the wild boar products of Macelleria Falorni (see p50) can be found in Via di Città. Most Siennese, though, buy food at the daily market, just behind the Campo in the Piazza del Mercato. Siena is known for its sweetmeats, especially *ricciarelli,* rich almondy, marzipan biscuits; *panforte* ('strong bread'); and *cantuccini,* crisp, almond-flavoured, almond-studded biscuits, ideal for dunking in Vin Santo.

PLACES OF INTEREST

The Campo

You can't not visit the Campo. It is probably Italy's most inspiring piazza and most streets ultimately lead you there.

The sloping, shell-shaped piazza is lower than its approaches so your first view is practically panoramic. The Campo is dominated by the 14th-century Palazzo Pubblico, topped by the Mangia tower. This symbolised the power of the laity against the power of the church and was craftily built just higher than the cathedral's tower. Unless a meal with a view is essential, do not be tempted to eat at the Campo, as you will pay heavily for the experience.

The Duomo

This is just a minute or so from the Campo. Some people adore the 13th-century striped cathedral, others loathe it. Either way, its Piazza is hardly big enough to do it justice.

The *Palio*

It seems impossible that a horse race, three times round the Campo and lasting just over a minute, can so dominate a city. Ten of the 17 *contrade* compete: the seven excluded the previous year plus three chosen by lot. Tales of skulduggery abound and the race itself is extremely dangerous. Not only are riders both suicidal and murderous in their intent to get round first, but there is a diabolical corner that can see some off. Still it is all accompanied by much feasting and the street dinners, before and after the event, are worth seeing if nothing else. Unless you have connections and get a place on a balcony overlooking the Campo, you are better off watching it on television. The *Palio* is held twice a year, in early July and in mid-August, with practice runs on the days before.

La Torre
Via Salicotto 7–9
Tel: 0577 287545
Simple, homely place for hearty appetites. Shared tables, cosmopolitan clientele. Basic but reasonable house wine: no list. No credit cards.

Vinaio Trombicche
Via delle Terme 66 *Tel: 0577 288089*
Good for snacks in city centre: salads, cheeses, *salumi*. Decent wine. Good for people-watching. Inexpensive but civilised.

FOOD AND WINE SHOPPING

Azienda Consorzio Provinciale Siena
Via Pianigiani
Wines and foods from the province.

Drogheria Manganelli
Via di Città 71/73
Extensive specialist grocers with over a century's history. Large selection of wine from the province.

Gastronomia Morbidi
Via Banchi di Sopra 75
Delicatessen famous for foods and dishes made on the premises.

Batelli
Via Cassia Nord 20, località Il Braccio
Outside the city but recommended. Terrific wood-oven-baked bread, cheeses and home-produced *salumi*.

La Nuova Pasticceria
Via Dupré 37
Wonderful *ricciarelli*.

La Pasticceria Buti
Via Vittorio Emanuele 37
Full of typical Sienese sweetmeats including *cantuccini* and *ricciarelli*.

Above *A romantic view of rural life around San Gimignano – a man stands at the gates to the town with his cows.*

SAN GIMIGNANO

RECOMMENDED PRODUCERS

Casale-Falchini
Tel: 0577 941305
Structured and perfumed Vernaccia, especially Riserva Vigna a Solatio. Also produces Paretaio (Sangiovese in barrique); highly rated Campora (Cabernet with a touch of Sangiovese); fruity Chianti Colli Senesi Titolato Colombaia; good Vin Santo.

Teruzzi e Puthod
Tel: 0577 940143
The estate is actually called **Fattoria Ponte a Rondolino**, but is known by the name of its owners, Enrico Teruzzi, a Milanese, and his French wife, Carmen Puthod. Carmen was a well known ballerina until a horse-riding accident ended her career. The couple came to San Gimignano to

San Gimignano

San Gimignano is the one place that does not fit conveniently into a round tour of Tuscany but it is still easily accessible. You could take a day out from Chianti Classico to see it, or visit from Florence or Siena, or from Volterra to the west. Whichever way, it can be reached in less than an hour. The 'city of towers' itself is so spectacular that it is tempting to see it sooner rather than later. And, although best known for its white wines, it lies within the Colli Senesi sub-zone of Chianti, so it is perhaps more logical to take it in before exploring further south and west.

GETTING THERE

Unless you approach from Volterra you will need to get through Poggibonsi, an ugly, semi-industrial town with nothing notable except frequent traffic jams. If coming up from Siena, take the old Via Cassia, the second state road created by Mussolini from Rome to Florence, through Siena. It is slower than the Florence – Siena *superstrada* but much prettier and gives superb views of the ancient castle of

Monteriggioni. Once past Poggibonsi the road leaves the Elsa valley and rises steadily, giving the first glimpses of San Gimignano.

There are now just 13 towers in the town although there were once more than 70. It seems that in San Gimignano in the middle ages, the higher your tower, the greater your prestige in the community, so each family tried to outdo its neighbours, building ever higher (with the inevitable occasional collapse). The towers also gave residents the means of spying on their neighbours and came in handy for launching missiles in the all too common event of a feud.

Top *On clear days distant mountains can be seen from San Gimignano.*
Above *A plaque adorning a cellar.*

THE WINE

Vernaccia is a white grape variety whose name can be roughly translated as 'belonging here' so it is not surprising that records show it growing in the area from the 13th century. Depending on how it is handled the wine can be deeply coloured, broad, rich and flat; or almost colourless, fresh, clean but rather neutral. The skill is in finding a balance between these two styles. Producers' ideas on that balance point vary and there are notable differences in the

overcome the trauma and started making wine for fun. It proved to be great therapy. Their wines became San Gimignano's best, and still are. Archetypal Vernaccia. Also Terre di Tufi (oaked Vernaccia), Carmen (also oaked white), Peperino (Sangiovese).

San Quirico
Tel: 0577 955007
Known for its fuller, traditionally styled Vernaccia, its wines are getting tighter, fresher and increasingly impressive, especially Riserva I Campi Santi.

Montenidoli
Tel: 0577 941565
Elisabetta Fagiuoli makes individual wines and recent developments have increased the number of admirers. three different types of Vernaccia: Fiore, from soft-pressed grapes; Tradizionale, from grape must given a short skin maceration before fermentation and Carato, which is fermented and matured in barrique. Also Chianti Colli Senesi, *rosato* from the variety Canaiolo; Sono Montenidoli, soft and elegant mainly from Sangiovese and others. *Agriturismo.*

Panizzi
Tel: 0577 941576
San Gimignano's rising star. Lovingly tended, high density, well sited vineyard, a thoughtfully equipped cellar and tons of enthusiasm from Giovanni Panizzi has resulted in wines many regard as the best in the area, especially the Vernaccia Riserva. Also: Chianti Colli Senesi.

ENOTECHE

Casa del Caffé
Via San Matteo
Just a few steps down the main street from Piazza Duomo on the right. Good selection of wines and olive oil, also bread, cheeses – just the place for picnic supplies. No tastings.

Da Gustavo
Via San Matteo
Further down on the left. The shop front says **Bar Enoteca Chianti Classico** but it has a carefully selected range of Italian wines, mainly Tuscan, including several Vernaccias, one of which is available for tasting daily. Other wines sold by the glass.

Above right *San Gimignano takes on a gentle, welcoming aspect in the rich light of early evening.*
Below *Flowers are plentiful in the charming town centre.*

wines' styles. Sadly, there are too many producers who still douse their wines with over-generous doses of sulphur dioxide, squashing the character of the wines even further, even though the wine is now DOCG. Many producers make red wine too; San Gimignano lies within the Chianti Colli Senesi zone, although not all opt to make use of this denomination.

THE VINEYARDS

Soon after spotting San Gimignano, you get glimpses of its first vineyards.

The estate Pietrafitta is the first, well signposted, although the cellars are off a small side-road to the right. Others quickly follow as you head up to the hill top town. The vineyards around Pietrafitta and those closest to the town should, in theory, produce the best wine but with Vernaccia the hand of the winemaker has a greater effect than small zonal fluctuations.

As the climb continues, the plots of vineyard become more dense and the city views more vivid. San Gimignano is, in fact, situated only a little over 300 metres above sea-level, but it seems much higher when viewed from a distance.

The charming centre is traffic-free, as in many Tuscan towns, but there are several car parks just outside. Or you can skirt the centre, keeping the city wall on your right, and just as you leave it behind there is a soft curve down with plenty of space to park on the verge. This is also the start-off point for a round tour of some of San Gimignano's idyllic, vine-dominated countryside.

Follow the road down in the direction of Certaldo to a Y-shaped junction where you fork left. Later the road sweeps round to the right in a large U-shape and leads towards Ulignano, passing the estates of Pietraserena (to the right), Casale-Falchini (left) and Teruzzi e Puthod's Ponte a Rondolino. At the next T-junction turn left (not to Ulignano) and continue winding downward to the next T-junction. There turn left again. This leads down to the northern extremity of the San Gimignano area by the Elsa valley, skirting Certaldo, where the difference between the pretty old town above and the down-at-heel town below

is a salutory lesson in town-planning. Then take a sharp U-turn southward, back up towards the town, passing Fattoria Il Paradiso, San Quirico (with the Pieve di Cellole nearby) and Le Colonne further up on the higher slopes. Half an hour should be enough time to complete the circuit, unless you stop frequently.

Within San Gimignano just walk, admire and enjoy. There are numerous cafes and restaurants in which to relax. On leaving it view the last main vineyard area by following the road round the town and heading out westward towards Montenidoli and Racciano. This non-asphalted road begins just to the left of a car park by a police station *(carabinieri)*. Follow the road down and over a small stream. Immediately to the left is Signano, Panizzi is a minute or so further on to the right and just a little past Panizzi a private road leads out to Montenidoli.

Back off the private road, continue to San Donato. There you can turn left onto an even rougher road and twist back round to Pietrafitta where you started, passing Canneta on the way. Alternatively, you can take the longer but easier route continuing south to the area's border at Castel San Gimignano, there turning left to Colle Vald'Elsa and the Florence–Siena roads, or right towards Volterra.

HOTELS

La Cisterna
Tel: 0577 940328
Right in the centre. Attractive outside, newly and comfortably furnished inside. Not expensive.

Sovestro
Tel: 0577 943153
New hotel just outside the town on the road to Poggibonsi. The estate Sovestro is adjacent.

Santa Chiava
Tel: 0577 940701

RESTAURANTS

Osteria delle Catene
Via Mainardi 18
Tel: 0577 941966
Highly recommended. Simply designed, relaxed *trattoria* serving well thought-out, traditionally based dishes. Good choice of Vernaccia di San Gimignano, Tuscan reds and Vin Santo to help down the *cantuccini*.

Dorandò
Vicolo dell'Oro 2
Tel: 0577 941862
Dishes based on old Medici recipes with some modern touches: good variety of flavours. Notable use of truffles and fruit. Tempting desserts. Fairly good wine list. Quite expensive.

Arnolfo
Colle Val d'Elsa
Tel: 0577 920549
San Gimignano lacks a good smart place but this one, outside the town, fills the breach. Choose between local and innovative tasting menus giving balanced and satisfying series of courses using first-rate ingredients. Good wine list. Fairly priced. Closed Tuesdays, mid-January to mid-February, first week in August.

FOOD SHOPPING

Buca di Montaiuto
Via San Giovanni 16
Good *salumi*, especially from wild boar.

PLACES OF INTEREST

Pieve di Cellole
This is a glorious little medieval church a few kilometres northwest of the town on the road to Certaldo, close to the estate San Quirico (turn left at signs to Il Castagno, San Vivaldo). A cypress-lined avenue leads to the simple church which was built with hand-worked stone. Off the beaten track, delightfully and refreshingly undisturbed by all the tourist hoards.

Arezzo and environs

AREZZO

RECOMMENDED PRODUCERS

Villa Cilnia
Pieve a'Bagnoro *Tel: 0575 365017*
The only producer near Arezzo of any worth. But, following a recent buy-out there has been instability. Steep, well aspected vineyards and an innovative approach. Range includes Chianti Colli Aretini, Le Vignacce (Cabernet, Sangiovese, Montepulciano), Vocato (Sangiovese/Cabernet), Campo del Sasso (Chardonnay/Malvasia Nera).

Fattoria Petrolo
Mercatale Valdarno *Tel: 055 9911322*
Small estate, lovingly produced elegant but well structured wines. Chianti 'Titolato', Torrione (Sangiovese), Vin Santo and others.

I Selvatici
Montevarchi *Tel: 055 901146*
Firmly structured wines from rapidly improving estate.

Fattoria di Ambra
Bucine *Tel: 055 996806*
Large estate, newly planted in 1988. Promising wines.

Villa la Selva
Bucine *Tel: 055 998203*
Owned by Sergio Carpini, industrialist

This is an optional extra, either as a round-about way of reaching Montepulciano or as a day-trip from Siena (just over an hour away). Arezzo is also in direct motorway contact with Florence. There is not a great deal of wine interest but is worth doing, as much for the beauty of the road as for the majesty of Arezzo itself.

From Siena, 20 minutes of travelling through gracious, soft hills bring you to the outskirts of Castelnuovo Berardenga. From there the road gets increasingly twisty and rises inexorably. The vines you see during the 15 minutes or so past the Castelnuovo turn off form part of Chianti Colli Senesi then, just before reaching the highest point of the road, you cross into the province of Arezzo and the occasional vines are Chianti Colli Aretini. The village below is Monte San Savino with a pretty medieval centre. From there, cross the dull Chiana Valley to reach Arezzo itself.

Arezzo is a calm, well-to-do town. The modern part is smart, with plentiful shopping; the important area, though, is the old town on the hill peak above with the large Medici fortress, a medieval/Renaissance cathedral, Santa Maria della Pieve, a glorious Romanesque church and Piero della Francesca frescoes in the Basilica of San Francesco.

From Arezzo you can tour the Casentino (see p30) or go on to Montepulciano. The *autostrada* is best. Exit at Val di Chiana, go through Bettolle to reach Torrita di Siena. You may see some white, horned Chianina cattle on the way – prized for their meat quality. The first vineyards you will see are Chianti Colli Aretini, most are Bianco Vergine

Below *Ancient coats-of-arms adorn Arezzo's Palazzo Pretorio.*

Left *The* campanile *(bell tower) of Arezzo's Santa Maria della Pieve church, half hidden behind one of its narrow, curving streets.*

Valdichiana. Otherwise take the road through Castiglion Fiorentino. There are more vineyards and terrific views over the Chiana valley from both medieval Castiglion Fiorentino and atmospheric Cortona, with its tiny, twisting streets high on a mountain ridge. Cortona is also medieval but has many Etruscan remains. Finally skirt the peaceful Lake Trasimeno (in Umbria) before turning right across the valley to Bettolle.

CHIANTI COLLI ARETINI

A Tuscan low-spot. Vineyards are sparse, often in poor condition, and few producers make anything of real worth. Some good estates have emerged recently, so the future looks brighter. The most promising part is on the Upper Arno's left bank, around Bucine, Mercatale and Montevarchi, next to Chianti Classico, about 30 minutes from Arezzo.

BIANCO VERGINE VALDICHIANA

Mainly Trebbiano with a little Malvasia, produced in the low hills of the Chiana valley. Often a light but uninspiring white, though a few producers make elegant, creamy, almondy wine.

turned winemaker. Lots of investment, and ready to make waves.

Fattoria di Manzano
Camucia (just south of Cortona)
Tel: 0575 618667
Huge investment in over 50ha of densely planted vineyard using traditional and innovative grape varieties. Exciting wines. An estate to watch. Bianco Vergine Valdichiana plus Vigna del Bosco (Syrah), Vigna del Vescovo (Gamay), Le Terrazze (Sauvignon).

RESTAURANTS

Buca di San Francesco
Via San Francesco 1 *Tel: 0575 23271*
Arezzo's most serious restaurant. Mainly classic Tuscan fare. Go for the food more than the wines. Closed Monday evening, Tuesday.

Il Cantuccio
Via Madonna del Prato 78
Tel: 0575 26830
Family-run *trattoria*. Soups a speciality. Produce their own Bianco Vergine Valdichiana, Chianti, Vin Santo, olive oil. Closed Wednesday.

L'Aganìa
Via Mazzini 10 *Tel: 0575 25381*
Traditional, rough and ready but friendly *trattoria*. House wine only. Inexpensive. Closed Monday.

FOOD SHOPPING

Arezzo is not great for food. Exceptions to dull shopping are:

Market (called 'Edin'): Saturday Viale Michelangiolo.

Pane e Salute
Corso Italia 11
Huge range of delicious breads.

Macelleria Gastronomia Aligi Barelli
Via della Chimera 20
Salumi and and great Chianina beef.

Veraldi
Via Calamandrei 154 – 156
Top-notch coffees

Torrefazione Artigiana Donatello
Via Vittorio Veneto 129
Fine range of coffees and teas.

SPECIAL EVENTS

Antiques fair
First Sunday of each month plus preceding Saturday.

Montepulciano

At just over 600 metres, Montepulciano is one of southern Tuscany's two major hill top wine towns. Standing high and cool it gives exhilarating views for miles across-country: San Quirico, over 15 kilometres away, is easily visible. The tufaceous soil under the town has been repeatedly burrowed into, from Etruscan times onward, and the caverns are still used by several estates as cellars, just as they have been for centuries. Imagine the effort involved in hauling barrels of fresh wine up the long inclines from the vineyards below to store them in the undisturbed, constant cool of the cellars; and then in bringing them back down once sold. Few who have the luxury of such premises use them as their everyday working cellars any more (Contucci is one who still does): it is too-labour intensive, and modern-day thinking requires wine to be moved as little as possible. Some of the cellars are open for visits, however; opening times are posted on plaques on the doors.

GETTING THERE

You may come into Montepulciano from Arezzo (see p78), but if starting from Siena follow the road to Perugia. Once you turn southeast, past the Arezzo turn-off, deep grey fissures begin to appear in the clay rock. These landmarks are known as *le crete di Siena*. Most of the vineyards you pass are Chianti Colli Senesi, which are liberally signposted as such. About half an hour out of Siena the major Farnetella estate is clearly sign-posted. A couple of minutes further along, fork right off the main road to Sinalunga, a small, functional town of no great interest, and within ten minutes you arrive in Torrita di Siena. Another couple of minutes (three kilometres) brings you into the commune of Montepulciano, where the wine zone also starts.

Left *Wandering up and down the narrow streets of Montepulciano it is startling to think that you are walking above networks of tunnels.* Above Crostata *partners sweet Vin Santo as well as* cantucci.

THE WINES

Montepulciano produces two wines, both from a blend dominated by Sangiovese (locally known as Prugnolo since the particular clone of the grape supposedly gives a plummy flavour) with Canaiolo, sometimes Mammolo, and, optionally, small quantities of the white grapes Trebbiano and Malvasia. The flagship is Vino Nobile di Montepulciano, DOCG, aged for a minimum of two years (three for the riserva). There is quite a difference in styles between producers. Some prefer more elegant, refined wines: 'wine for the nobles'; others prefer intense, slow-ageing blockbusters: 'noble wines'. Either way, from very shaky beginnings when the wines became DOCG 15 years ago, there have been massive improvements. Now, replacing a communal chip on the shoulder is a buzz of confidence and sense of direction. Part of the reason for the upsurge in consistency of quality in Vino Nobile was the introduction of the second wine, the DOC Rosso di Montepulciano. Not only did it satisfy the need for a more youthful, fruitier style, but it helped ensure that only the best grapes went into Vino Nobile.

The soil in Montepulciano is generally loamy; a good mixture of clay, limestone and sand, interspersed with marine deposits from old tributaries of the Chiana.

Some producers also make Chianti Colli Senesi and those with vineyards in the extreme east of the zone may also produce Bianco Vergine Valdichiana.

THE VINEYARDS

As you start to rise into Montepulciano you are surrounded by three of the area's best sub-zones; Ascianello to the right, Abbadia to the left and Gracciano ahead. Continue towards Gracciano. This is the starting point for the tour which is in two stages, two large loops, each taking a good hour.

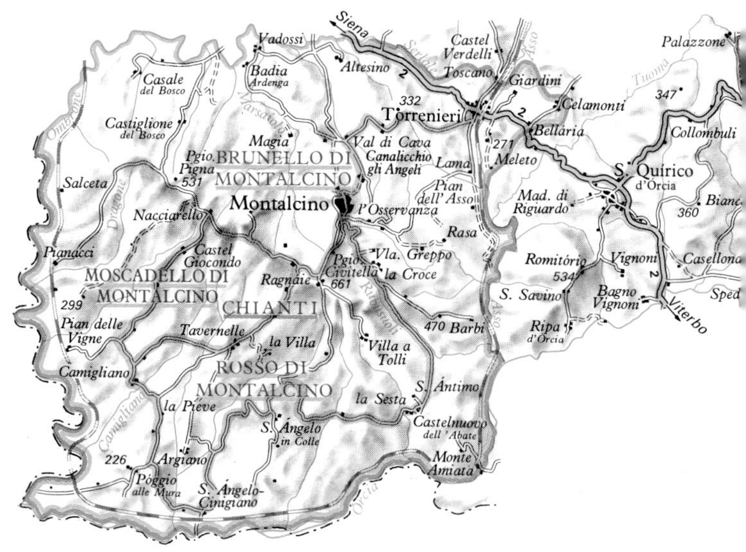

Above *The dominating Palazzo Communale in Montepulciano.*

Above *Small shops still play a major role in Italian towns.*
Right *Colourful banners in Montepulciano.*
Far right *A powerful view of the town from its surroundings.*

CHIANTI COLLI SENESI

RECOMMENDED PRODUCERS

Castello di Farnetella
Tel: 0576 663520
Run by Giuseppe Mazzocolin who also controls the magnificent Felsina in Chianti Classico, aided by consultant winemaker Franco Bernabei. Terrific Chianti Colli Senesi and classy international varietals.

Most other good Chianti Colli Senesi comes from estates in Montepulciano and Montalcino.

MONTEPULCIANO

RECOMMENDED PRODUCERS

Unless stated otherwise, all those listed below produce both Vino Nobile di Montepulciano and Rosso di Montepulciano.

Avignonesi*
Tel: 0578 757872/3
English spoken. Enormous, powerful mouth-fillers of intensity, weight, extract and class which take years to mature. Besides Le Cappezzine the Avignonesi brothers have estates at Poggetti and La Selva. Also produce Grifi (Sangiovese, Cabernet), Marzocco (acclaimed *barrique* Chardonnay), Il Vignola (Sauvignon), Merlot, Aleatico di Sovano, Rosso Avignonesi and Bianco Avignonesi. Plus the most intense, long-aged, nectar-like (and expensive) Vin Santo you'll ever be lucky enough to taste.

NORTHEAST MONTEPULCIANO

At Gracciano, turn left towards Valiano, passing, in quick succession, the estates Raspanti (to the left), the 18th-century Tenuta di Gracciano (left), with next door Fattoria di Gracciano followed by Fattoria di Mazzuchelli. The next modern building to the right is Poliziano. From here you descend to 250 metres, below which Montepulciano wines may not be produced, and suddenly the vineyards all but disappear. The few you see are for Bianco Vergine Valdichiana. There are remnants of *la fila*, the 18th-century system of looping vines along field boundaries. Now follow the road to the right and across the broad Chiana valley to Valiano, a separate Montepulciano sub-zone.

To the right is Lodera Nuova, followed by Tenute Trerose, a huge modern estate. You are in a small spur of

Montepulciano between the province of Arezzo (left) and the border of Tuscany with Umbria. Up ahead, slightly to the right, is the Fattoria delle Capezzine, one of three estates belonging to the Avignonesi and incorporating their barrique cellar plus another storing their much-lauded Vin Santo.

Continuing to Le Capezzine, La Calonica is just visible over a hillock to the far right. By the next small junction you are at the far extreme of Montepulciano, 15 minutes of fast driving from Gracciano. Either turn back or take a sharp right and loop back onto this road behind Trerose.

At the three-way junction just past the second railway line, fork slightly left (signposted Montepulciano). This goes behind Poliziano (right) and Nottola (right). At the next junction bend right (direction Sinalunga) and within seconds you are back at Gracciano. Now turn sharp left, signposted Fassati, and in one minute Fassati's cellars appear on the left and their vineyards on the right, with Montefollonico high up. Go on and the Salarco stream flows parallel on the right. The vineyards are Le Caggiole's, growing white grapes on the flatter land and red above, while to the right are those of Innocenti. All these are within a couple of kilometres, before the next junction. Ahead and to the left are the lands of Contucci, while round the corner is the Asinone vineyard, a special *cru* of Poliziano.

At the next T-junction go right back on to the main road. At the next junction, slip left by the Consorzio Agrario then immediately right into Via dei Canneti. This takes you under Montepulciano. Follow round (keeping the town on the left). You pass the

Terre di Bindella*
Tel: 0578 767777
Owned by Swiss Rudolf Bindella. Everything based on detailed research, technology and investment: Montepulciano's most densely planted vineyard (over 9000 vines/ha); small barrels kept in air-conditioned cellars. Slow developing, firm, structured wines.

Poderi Boscarelli*
Tel: 0578 767608
Smallish, well-sited, excellently exposed vineyards. Rich, powerful wines, strong aromas, fruit, body and backbone yet elegant. Also produces Boscarelli (intense Sangiovese and Cabernet), Chianti Colli Senesi.

La Calonica
Tel: 0578 724119
At extreme northeastern edge of the zone, near Lake Trasimeno which creates its own microclimate, tempering winter cold and summer heat and assisting humidity. Traditional leanings, well typed wines. Also produces Chianti Colli Senesi, Bianco Vergine Valdichiana, Vin Santo.

Canneto estate and then emerge beside the San Biagio church. Turn right. For views of both church and town, turn right again and go for about one kilometre, past Cantina Santavenere. Otherwise turn left, until you have come full circle, back to the Consorzio Agrario. Now, at last, you can go up to the town, park, and, on foot, experience its fascination.

EAST MONTEPULCIANO

Leave Montepulciano along the road to Chianciano Terme. Follow it until it U-bends to the right. Here go straight ahead on a minor road towards Argiano. This is the heart of Montepulciano. Passing woods on the left you see Fattoria di Paterno, then a large stretch of vineyard belonging to Fattoria del Cerro. Notice the difference between the older plots with fewer vines and the new plots which, for higher quality, have greater vine density. Fattoria del Cerro's cellars are the low, pink, dark-roofed buildings on the left. Off to the right is Le Casalte with Montepulciano's best-kept vineyards. The next stage is probably the most unspoilt part, with old cultivation systems still in evidence. Keep curving down (ignore the left fork to Argiano itself) until

Agricola Canneto
Tel: 0578 757737
Almost 20ha of vineyard. Owned by Swiss and most of production is exported. Neat vineyards and recently re-equipped cellar bode well and wines are rounded and balanced.

Fattoria Le Casalte*
Tel: 0578 799138
Gem of an estate. Guido Barioffi is passionate about grape-growing and his vineyards are among the most perfect in Tuscany. A consultant winemaker helps him express in the wines the flavours he has coaxed into the grapes. Also grows Chardonnay and Grechetto.

Contucci*
Tel 0578 757006
Strange mix of modern wines and an ancient cellar. Need good vintages to express their character.

Dei
Tel 0578 716878
New company – 1985 was the first vintage. Prime exponent of lighter, fruitier, more elegant Vino Nobile.

Fattoria del Cerro*
Tel: 0578 767722
Large, impressive estate. Some 120ha of productive vineyard with 560ha of new plantings. In the forefront of viticultural experimentation. Produces rich, fruity wines with good body especially Vino Nobile cru, Vigneto Antica Chiusina. Broad portfolio.

Fassati
Tel 0578 708705
Large company with huge, well ordered cellars. Tirelessly enthusiastic director Amedeo Esposito heads the

Above *Old* casa colonica.
Right *Flagons such as these have almost disappeared from Tuscany's wine zones.*
Far right *An ancient olive tree.*

you leave the cultivation zone, crossing under the motorway and turning left onto the main road. On the left is a cypress-lined avenue to Poggio alla Sala. (This stretch takes 15–25 minutes.) Now take the main road for five minutes and just after crossing the motorway you reach Acquaviva. In the middle of this village turn left into a narrow street, towards Cervognano. Most *agriturismo* centres are located in this area.

An avenue on the right leads to the pretty estate of Poderi Boscarelli. A couple of minutes later you pass the hamlet of Cervognano and, three or four minutes after that, the estate Fanetti (right). At the junction that follows either detour left to see the vineyards of Dei, or continue rightish. Seconds later, U-curve to the right onto a non-asphalted road, the Strada di Bossona. (On maps, the road appears to stop at Bossona but it does continue.) The next batch of vineyards on the right is the German-owned Il Conventino. The road descends to a cross-roads, the area of Tenuta Valdipiatta. Straight ahead are a few shacks, so turn right, onto a rutted track until the T-junction where you turn left, back onto asphalted road. At the next junction (with road signs) turn left to return to Montepulciano.

operation. Wines have been inconsistent but super-consultant Franco Bernabei has been seconded and there are already leaps forward.

Fattoria di Gracciano
Tel: 0578 708228
Reliable, concentrated, slow-maturing, wines from old vines. Rounded, floral Vin Santo and Bianco del Paladino (Trebbiano, Malvasia, Grechetto).

Vittorio Innocenti
Tel: 0578 669537
Smallish estate with land straddling Montepulciano border so a third of production is Vino Nobile or Rosso di Montepulciano, most of the rest Chianti Colli Senesi. Wines are classic; clean, well perfumed with a firm tannic backbone and class.

Poliziano*
Tel: 0578738171
Some 80ha of vineyard on three sites: at Gracciano, Le Caggiole and Le Pietrose. Intense, powerful wines. Owner Federico Carletti is one of the few to select different plots for Rosso di Montalcino rather than making a selection of grapes. Vino Nobile cru Vigna Asinone is the standard-bearer. Also makes Elegia (Sangiovese and Cabernet), Le Stanze (Cabernet Sauvignon), Vin Santo.

Tenuta Trerose*
Tel: 0578 724018
Large, modernistic estate. Well made wine including a series of whites.

Tenuta Valdipiatta*
Tel: 0578 757930
A small, enthusiastic family-run estate. The wines improve each year and have individuality, power and elegance.

* For more information on the estates marked with an asterisk and/or Fattoria La Braccesca, Tenimenti Ruffino and Talosa, contact Maddalena Mazzeschi (*tel: 0578 758465*), who deals with public relations for the group.

Above *Newly bottled wine awaits release for sale.*
Right and below right *The vine-dominated landscape around Montepulciano and Montalcino.*
Centre *'Poliziano' was the ancient name for Montepulciano.*
Far right *Wooden stakes, used to support the wires in the vineyard.*

HOTELS

Unless staying in Siena or Arezzo, it is best to stay at La Chiusa at Montefollonico or at Locanda dell'Amorosa (see below). Or go to San Quirico (see p89).

RESTAURANTS

Locanda dell'Amorosa
località Amorosa, Sinalunga
Tel: 0577 679497
Appositely named: whether eating inside or out, you feel relaxed and cosseted. Inventive dishes with a Tuscan base. Comfortable rooms. Closed Mondays, Tuesday lunchtime.

La Chiusa
Montefollonico *Tel: 0577 669668*
Top-notch, smart (and expensive). Food based on local ingredients but light and balanced. Closed Tuesdays.

Diva e Maceo
Montepulciano *Tel: 0578 716951*
Classic fare and good choice of local wines. Crowded. Closed Tuesdays. Excellent value. Cash only.

MONTEPULCIANO TO MONTALCINO

The drive between Montepulciano and its fellow hill top wine town Montalcino is not only one of Tuscany's most beautiful roads but shows clearly how viticulture and other land use follow the natural suitability of the teritory.

From Montepulciano, head towards Pienza. Vineyards gradually diminish but, even after leaving the wine zone (contiguous with the commune), there are still some vines around, belonging to Chianti Colli Senesi. Through this attractive stretch of rolling hills cultivation is more varied, with plots of fruit, vegetables and grazing areas for sheep.

PIENZA

Within 15 minutes you arrive at Pienza. It is well worth a stroll round the old centre, in particular the main piazza, with its decorated alcoves. For further tranquillity, visit the Pieve di Corsignano, a peaceful, simple Romanesque church just outside the town. Pienza is renowned for its cheeses: ricotta and the locally famous pecorino di Pienza, and a speciality biscuit named after Lucrezia Borgia.

From Pienza the road descends once more into a huge, exhilarating stretch of open countryside. Within ten minutes it rises again, towards the small, smart town of San Quirico Val d'Orcia and going through this leads to Bagno Vignoni. This is a popular spa resort where hot springs gush out at 40°C. Some of the pools are even open at night on summer weekends.

To reach Montalcino, skirt San Quirico in the direction of Siena. Soon there are the first signs of the famous weirdly evocative 'moonscape' of blue-grey clay that dominates much of southwestern Tuscany. Within five minutes, at Torrenieri, Montalcino is signposted off the main road. Vineyards begin to reappear and suddenly, there is Montalcino, at just under 600 metres high, astride a huge massif – one of Tuscany's most awe-inspiring sights.

Pulcino
Montepulciano *Tel: 0578 757242*
An experience! This huge 'Ristorante Rustico' is set among vines and olives on the road leading southeast from the town. You sit at long bench tables to enjoy huge portions of hearty fare.

FOOD SHOPPING

Market day: Thursday
Caseificio Silvana Cugusi
Via Gracciano del Corso 31
For local cheese, Pecorino di Pienza

PLACES OF INTEREST

Enoteca Oinochoé
Via di Voltaia nel Corso 82
Large selection of wines from all Italy.
Cantina del Redi
The most exciting of the underground cellars. Probably Etruscan dating from the 14th century. Some parts of vast height, others very low. Small shop with wines, small selection of foodstuffs, ceramics.
Antico Caffé Poliziano
Via di Voltaia nel Corso.
A must. The most elegant bar in the province. Established 1868. Good coffee, snacks and extensive views.

PIENZA AND SAN QUIRICO

HOTELS

Hotel Residence Casanova
San Quirico
Tel: 0577 898177
A haven. Spacious, refined, restful, designed in typical Tuscan style but all mod cons. Swimming pool.

PIENZA AND SAN QUIRICO

(CONTINUED)

Hotel Posta
Bagno Vignoni Tel: 0577 887112
Steaming natural swimming pool: bubbling hot water (40°C).

RESTAURANTS

La Buca delle Fate
Pienza *Tel: 0578 748448*
Long bench tables, homely cooking. Classic Tuscan dishes. Montepulciano wines in carafe, also by the glass at the bar. Closed Mondays.

Taverna di Moranda
Monticchello (Pienza)
Tel: 0578 755050
Smart but inexpensive traditional fare. Great local wine list. Closed Mondays.

Osteria del Leone
Bagno Vignoni, San Quirico
Tel: 0577 887300
Tasty, substantial dishes, traditional. Good local wine list. Not costly. Closed Mondays.

MONTALCINO

RECOMMENDED PRODUCERS

Unless stated otherwise, all those listed below produce Brunello di Montalcino and Rosso di Montalcino. 'Brunello' on its own refers to the grape.

Tenuta di Argiano
Tel: 0577 864037
Owned by Cinzano but run locally. Beautiful villa with commanding views and wonderful, old, barrel-lined cellars. Wines broad, powerful, concentrated and with personality.

Altesino
Tel: 0577 806208
Fine modernist estate with some 100ha of land but smallish vineyard sites at Altesino, Montosoli and

Montalcino

Wine seems to ooze from the pores of Montalcino. There are what would otherwise be far too many enoteche for such a small place; bars boast dozens of labels, as does even the simplest trattoria. The square beneath the fortress, the town's focal point, is even adorned with a giant plaque, courtesy of the Brunello di Montalcino Consorzio, listing its estates and marking them on a map.

Yet Montalcino's wine history is relatively recent. Although produced here for centuries, it is only in the past 125 years that its wines have become such a talking-point. It is not clear how interest in Montalcino took off. The much-repeated story is that the Biondi-Santi family developed the Brunello grape (a particular Sangiovese clone) and by using it unblended, created the wine's style and quality. However, numerous luminaries dispute this and produce equally convincing evidence to support their version of events. Whatever the truth, few other areas in Italy have sustained such consistently high quality with their wines.

GETTING THERE

Montalcino is just half an hour from Montepulciano and less than an hour from Siena. A fair bit of the route from Siena takes you along the old Via Cassia but, slowly, by-passes and dual-carriageway stretches are being built to ease congestion.

Above *Pienza was developed in the Renaissance and was one of the first experiments in town-planning.* Left *Grappa, Italy's equivalent of the French brandy* marc, *is made from the skins and pips of grapes from which wine has been made.*

The road follows the Arbia valley. These lands are fertile and grow cereals and fruits. There is also plentiful grazing land for sheep and Chianina cattle. It is a comparatively boring stretch so it is a relief to reach Buoncenvento, where the Arbia flows into the Ombrone, south Tuscany's most important river, since just past the town you see Montalcino signposted. Within a minute or two you cross the borders of the zone. The road curves and suddenly, Montalcino astride its hill is in view, a breathtaking sight. The scenery as you rise is stupendous – photographs never do justice to its often misty, softly coloured, wide expanses.

THE WINES

Montalcino's reputation hangs on Brunello di Montalcino (DOCG), made exclusively from the Brunello grape, a Sangiovese clone. It is aged a minimum four years, at least the first three of which are in wood. It is slow-maturing and long-lived giving big richly fruited, powerful, intensely flavoursome, complex red wines. If proof were needed that Sangiovese is capable of producing some of the world's top wines, Brunello di Montalcino would be it. Nearly all producers also make Rosso di Montalcino (DOC), also exclusively from Brunello: it is younger (one year's minimum ageing), livelier, less intense and more overtly fruity, yet still stylish and fairly concentrated.

In recent years there has also been a revival of Moscadello di Montalcino. The white Moscadello grape is a version of

Gauggiole. Wines restrained, elegant, supple and fruit-forward. Also: Palazzo Altesi (Brunello in *barrique)*, Alte Altesi (Brunello and Cabernet).

Banfi
Tel: 0577 840111
Huge estate developed by the massive Banfi corporation, American importers of Italian wine. Over 800ha of vines of which 150ha produce Brunello di Montalcino, and one of Italy's largest cellars, a stainless steel palace linked to a palace of oak. Numerous wines including international varieties as well as Brunello or Brunello blends. The top Brunello di Montalcino Riservas are faultless examples of the denomination style, even if they are rather lacking in individuality.

Fattoria dei Barbi
Tel: 0577 848277
One of Montalcino's most high-profile estates, run by Francesca Colombini Cinelli and her daughter. Older vintages variable, recent ones more promising. Brunello di Montalcino Riserva 'Vigna del Fiore' leads the range. Also Brusco dei Barbi, Bruscone dei Barbi, Moscadello di Montalcino, Vin Santo.

Biondi-Santi
Tel: 0577 847121
Top-quality reputation. Strangely resistant to increasing numbers of doubting voices. Do not expect an open house. The best you can expect is a taste of their most recent Rosso di Montalcino, if you are lucky.

Tenuta Caparzo
Tel: 0577 848390
English, German spoken. Vineyards at Torrenieri, La Caduta, and La Casa. Open, rounded wines but need time to soften. They also make Ca' del Pazzo (Sangiovese and Cabernet), Le Grance (Chardonnay) and others; olive oil.

Casanova di Neri
Tel: 0577 834029
Concentrated, warm, well structured wines of great richness, especially Riserva 'Cerretalto'.

Case Basse
Tel: 0577 848567
Top estate. Award-winning, huge, concentrated structured wines. Also Inistieti, from the same grape grown on his best site but earlier-bottled than the Brunello di Montalcino.

Tenuta di Castelgiocondo
Tel: 0577 848492
English, German, French spoken. Large estate producing comparatively

Moscato Bianco and produces light, fresh and refreshing, wonderfully grapey and gently sweet wines. There are three styles: still, *frizzante* (slightly sparkling) and *vendemmia tardiva* (late harvest). The last, made from grapes picked later than normal to increase ripeness and sometimes left to dry a short while to concentrate them further, is stronger and fuller flavoured. Producers differ as to which type represents the 'true' Moscadello and rarely make more than one style.

THE VINEYARDS

Montalcino's vineyard area is bounded by three rivers: the Orcia, the Asso and the Ombrone. It also divides naturally into three sub-zones. Vineyards to the north tend to produce lighter, more elegant wines; those to the east, sheltered from the prevailing weather systems, are more structured and firmer while those to the warmer south, where the Mediterranean exerts a gently moderating influence, make the biggest, richest, most powerful wines. It is logical to see the estates in these three groupings.

NORTH MONTALCINO

Estates are quite clustered to the north and can be seen in a little over half an hour. All normal roads out of Montalcino leave from just under the

Top *Tuscan meals often finish off simply with fresh seasonal fruit such as figs.*
Above *Workers busily produce Pecorino cheese at Fattoria dei Barbi.*
Right *La Fiaschetteria, the meeting place in Montalcino, with a fantastic cellar of wines.*

Fortezza at the south end of town, but you need to leave from the north through the Porta Burelli and descend steeply on a heavenly, non-asphalted road. Go through the gate-posts ahead then turn right at the next T-junction. This leads onto the hill of Montosoli, with vineyards belonging to Altesino and others. You pass those of Capanna di Cencione and, after a curve to the left, 'La Casa', a cru of Tenuta di Caparzo, appears on the hill to the left.

After a large bend to the right, the Valdicava estate appears (on the right). Seconds later, turn left and right in quick succession (call this spot Point A) and all signs of vine cultivation vanish. Two minutes later Torrenieri (Montalcino's threshold and the site of Casanova di Neri) is signposted to the right. Do not take it: keep going straight until a fork, then go left (the white house you can see to the left is Altesino). You pass Tenuta di Caparzo along a cypress-lined lane, followed by Altesino.

Another big curve to the left and you are almost at the zone's edge. Turn left at the 'Stop' sign, and head back up southwards. Shortly you are back at Point A (see above). Continue up into Montalcino heartland. The scenery around here is dominated by the Val di Suga estate. Once

Top *Sun shines on Montalcino town, which is packed with enoteche, bars and restaurants offering good ranges of wines.* Above *Cypresses lead up to Tenuta Col d'Orcia.*

light but richly fruited and good-value Brunello di Montalcino and soft, delicious Rosso di Montalcino. The estate's direction is slowly changing to firmer, concentrated and yet more elegant wines, without losing fruit. One to watch. Also produces Vergena (barriqued Sauvignon) and Lamaione (Merlot), grappa, olive oil.

Cerbaiona
Tel: 0577 848660
Jewel of an estate; small, family-run with, in good vintages, superb, full, supple but well structured wines. Also makes Cerbaiona Rosso (Brunello, earlier-bottled).

Chiesa di Santa Restituta
Tel: 0577 848610
Beautifully tended vineyards, an excellent site, a dedicated winemaker and the help of renowned consultant Angelo Gaja combine to produce big, rich, firm, concentrated wines.

Col d'Orcia
Tel: 0577 808004
Great stuff! Warmth and richness with superb refinement. Owned by Cinzano but run locally by small, proficient team. Top wine Brunello di Montalcino Riserva 'Poggio al Vento' is a stunner; the Rosso di Montalcino an easy-drinking delight. Excellent Moscadello.

Costanti
Tel: 0577 848195
The estate is actually called **Colle al Matrichese** but is known by the owner's name, Andrea Costanti. Firm, elegant and remarkably classy wines:

the Rosso di Montalcino just as much as the Brunello di Montalcino. Also makes Vermiglio (also Brunello).

Greppone Mazzi
Tel: 0577 849215
Owned by Ruffino, the large Chianti company. Apart from Moscadello di Montalcino, produces only Brunello di Montalcino Riserva, aged five years plus. Warm, fat, traditional wines.

Lisini
Tel: 0577 864040
Lean, firm wines that need coaxing to show their character. Once they do, the refinement, full fruit and spiciness make the wait worthwhile.

Pian di Conte
Tel: 0577 864029
Pierluigi Talenti, having spent his working life turning Il Poggione's wines into some of the area's best, certainly could not do any less with his own property now that he is in retirement. Fabulous, superbly balanced and consistent wine.

Il Poggione
Tel: 0577 864029
The essence of Montalcino. Large, powerful, complex, long-lasting wines. Winemaker Fabrizio Bindocci, who worked with Talenti (see above) is fearsomley jealous of Il Poggione's reputation – the best way to ensure its perpetuation. Don't leave the area without trying some. Also Moscadelle.

Poggio Antico
Tel: 0577 848044
Large estate with well exposed and well tended vineyard. Restrained, elegant wines of great style.

Tenuta Valdicava
Tel: 0577 848261
Renovated cellars and vineyard have transformed the wines; soft with rounded fruit, concentration and structure. An estate to watch.

Above *Castello Banfi, now owned by huge American corporation Banfi.*
Below *Montalcino's vineyards have increased greatly in the last 20 years.*

past its flag-bedecked buildings and immaculate vineyards, take the next right onto a narrow, steep, unmade road. This is the Canalicchio and marks another area densely populated with estates: Canalicchio di Sotto, Canalicchio di Sopra, La Gerla and others. In a cloud of dust the road levels out and you are back at the beginning of the circuit.

EAST MONTALCINO

The eastern estates are even more densely packed than those to the north and can be seen in about 20 minutes. This time leave the town from under the fortress. Take the extreme left of the roads in front (direction Siena) and head down, with a huge left curve just by a large enoteca. Follow this road until the next junction then fork right. Az Costanti is on the right with Greppone Mazzi behind.

Take the next right fork too, on an unmade road, through a group of tiny estates, Fornacella, Fornacina and La Fornace (clearly once the site of an important furnace). From there keep left and drive for a couple of minutes along a pretty, peaceful road. The views are good too with the towers of San Quirico and

Left *Slow maturing and long-lived, Brunello di Montalcino is aged a minimum four years, at least the first three of which are in wood.*
Below *Fattoria dei Barbi, one of Montalcino's most high-profile estates.*

Val di Suga
Tel: 0577 848701
Large, modern estate. Wines of high quality, classically typed, with good fruit. Recent change in ownership, so changes may occur.

HOTELS

Al Brunello di Montalcino
Località Bellaria. *Tel: 0577 849304*
Modern, comfortable, but rather cramped rooms. The hotel restaurant is smart and not at all bad.

Pienza in the distance. Practically the last house you come to is San Filippo, an attractive place surrounded by its own veinyards, before the road comes to an end. Turn back on yourself and at the second junction (with signposts to several estates) swing round to the right. The huge oak tree on the right signals the entrance to La Fortuna, a small estate making pretty good, if rather unpolished, wines. Within a minute or so you leave east Montalcino, marked by the Canalicchio track (with a clump of signs) to the left. Take this to get back up to town.

NB: Mid-1995 three hotels were in construction. Two should be open by 1996. Check with tourist office, (also for *agriturismi*) *Tel: 0577 849331.*

SOUTH MONTALCINO

The estates of south Montalcino are widely spaced and to see the area properly takes about one and a half hours. It is, though, Montalcino's most gloriously beautiful part and worth dallying over. Leave town from under the fortress, taking the middle road signposted to Castelnuovo dell'Abate. Three minutes on is a clump of trees to the left with a cypress avenue leading from it. This is Il Greppo, Biondi-Santi's estate. Then, past a relatively flat area, an avenue on the left leads to Fattoria dei Barbi. By now, weather permitting, there should be good views of Mount Amiata ahead. There are the first sights of Mediterranean scrub among the trees, a sure sign that this zone is considerably warmer than any you have been through so far.

The next interest spot is Sant'Antimo, a marvellously simple, tranquil 12th-century church that appears, seemingly out of nowhere. Follow the road under Castelnuovo dell'Abate through wild, forested countryside, interspersed

RESTAURANTS

Sciame
Tel: 0577 848017
Just down from the fortress, halfway between trattoria and restaurant with prices on the low side. Typical Tuscan specialities. Mid-length wine list with good range of Montalcino wines.

Il Pozzo
Sant'Angelo in Colle
Tel: 0577 864015
Mouthwatering, well-flavoured wholesome Tuscan dishes. Great olive oil; plentiful selection of local wines.

La Taverna dei Barbi
Tel: 0577 849357
Meals and snacks on the Fattoria dei Barbi estate. Closed Wednesdays.

Test bottles (above) *lie maturing at Biondi Santi* (centre).
Far right (top). *The crumbling* casa colonica *near Montalcino.*
Far right (bottom) *Gleaming stainless steel vats at Tenuta Col d'Orcia.*

with vineyard patches and olive trees, some very old. The village on the hill ahead is Sant'Angelo in Colle and approaching it, you are in some of the southernmost lands of the zone. Much of it belongs to Il Poggione.

Asphalt returns at the next T-junction. Turning right would lead back to Montalcino, but instead turn left and follow the road beneath Sant'Angelo in Colle. It is worth diverting up into this peaceful village, not just for the Trattoria Il Pozzo but also for the stunning views over southern Montalcino including the full extent of the Banfi vineyards (see below). Back down on the main road, the first estate to the right is Pian di Conte, a retirement present given by Il Poggione to their much-loved and talented winemaker, the aptly named Talenti.

The next junction, *Bivio Argiano,* is named after the estate there, one of the zone's most imposing buildings. Five minutes out of Sant'Angelo in Colle you come to Sant'Angelo Scalo, a rather dull village. Pass through it to see the anything but dull Col d'Orcia. Sant'Angelo Scalo marks Montalcino's southern boundary but there is still much more to see so swing right and head back northward.

The massive complex down to the left is the headquarters of Banfi. For the next 15 minutes, perfectly serried

Poggio Antico
Tel: 0577 849200
This is where to go when you want a break from typical Tuscan. Smart restaurant on the Poggio Antico estate. Delicate, beautifully flavoured dishes including Lake Trasimeno fish. Eclectic choice of wines but, reasonably, the only Montalcino is Poggio Antico. Terrific value.

ENOTECHE

La Fiaschetteria
Piazza del Popolo
The meeting place in Montalcino and not to be missed. Behind the bar is an Aladdin's cave of wine with bins for most of the best Brunello and

vines eerily fill the landscape – so unlike anywhere else in Montalcino – and practically all belong to the huge Banfi territory. To the left is the castle of Poggio alle Mura, also owned by Banfi and completely (and expensively) restored by them. Apart from its use for major dinners and entertaining, it holds an enthralling and valuable collection of antique wine bottles and glasses, which is open to the public.

A few minutes later is the hamlet of Camigliano, with the eponymous estate down to the left. At this point you feel as if you are travelling though a large vineyard saucer, rimmed by hills. The highpoint of this rim is to the west (left), the hill top town of Roccastrada. On the right is a neat plantation of young oaks: a Banfi experiment where they have injected truffle spores into the roots to see if they can cultivate truffles. A further few minutes brings you to the edge of the village Tavernelle. At this point a side road (left) will take you to Castelgiocondo. Just past the village another side road (to the right), leads to a series of estates. You will recognise this from the great column of road signs, all facing the other direction. Take this right turn for a five-minute diversion to Caprili, the first estate to the left, through foresting; Case Basse, literally 'two low houses 'straddling the road which passes between them; and Chiesa di Santa Restituta, whose vineyards surround the ancient church.

Back on the main road the more normal mixed cultivation returns and you pass Tenuta Friggiali on the left. Less than five minutes brings you to a T-junction, at which point you are just another five minutes from the town reached by turning right, then turning left at the junction which follows shortly after. Alternatively you could turn right here (especially if you are hungry), to travel back south a short way to the estate and restaurant of Poggio Antico.

Rosso di Montalcino and many of the best Chiantis too. Snacks served.

Enoteca della Fortezza
Piazzale della Fortezza
Run by a true wine enthusiast. Full selection of local wines. Small range of fine wines from outside Tuscany.

Enoteca Franci
Via Ricasoli, Cantaste
Just across the road from the *trattoria* Sciame. Wide range of wines.

SPECIAL EVENTS

Honey week
First weekend of September: everything to do with honey.

PLACES OF INTEREST

The Fortezza
Tel: 0577 849211
Huge collection of Montalcino wines available for tasting, drinking and buying. Panoramic views. Light snacks available. Eccentrically, it is closed at lunchtime from 1.00 – 2.00pm.

RA 3673 D
IM 2127D
GIN DRY

Grosseto and the Maremma

After Chianti Classico, Montepulciano and Montalcino, you may think you have seen the best of Tuscany. You have a surprise in store. There may be few other areas with as much vineyard land, but as far as natural beauty is concerned there is plenty to see, some, if anything, more glorious than before. And a few outcrops of vineyard in an otherwise non-vine vista can catch the spirit of viticultural endeavour even more powerfully.

You could leave Montalcino via Sant'Antimo and drive on a series of tiny, twisty roads past Mount Amiata towards Acquapendente and Lake Bolsena. Or you could take the Via Cassia to the same places from San Quirico. The scenery is wonderful on the smaller roads, but the route is long and almost entirely vine free.

To keep the wine theme alive, the best route is to go straight to Grosseto, in the southwest of the region, and use it as a base for exploring the southern Tuscan wine zones. Cross out of the Montalcino zone at Sant'Angelo Scalo, and turn right immediately after crossing the River Orcia. From here you are in Grosseto's province, and in less than an hour, in the town itself.

ARCIDOSSO AND MOUNT AMIATA

This is an optional add-on but gives you a rich taste of the diversity of the Southern Tuscan countryside and a 'secret' wine zone. After crossing the River Orcia turn left and head to Arcidosso. After a few minutes, you suddenly plunge into a wild landscape covered with Mediterranean scrub. These are on the lower slopes of Mount Amiata, which soars up

Left *Punta Ala on the Grosseto coast. An additional bonus of Grosseto town is that it is a short hop through cool pine forests to the sea, with beaches at Marina de Grosseto and Principine a Mare.*

Right *Food in the Maremma generally follows Tuscan norms, with cheeses, well flavoured pasta and delicious game when in season.*

GROSSETO

HOTELS PRODUCERS

I Due Pini
Tel: 0564 34607 (Marina di Grosseto)
Run by Grosseto's leading trainer of sommeliers so wine plays a leading role; homely, family-run hotel. Garden.

Nuovo Grosseto
Tel: 0564 414105
Just by the station. Solid old building, recently completely renovated; run with charm and professionalism. Spotlessly clean and comfortable.

RESTAURANTS

Il Canto del Gallo
Grosseto *Tel: 0564 414589*
A tiny place tucked into the city walls. Food seasonal, abundant vegetables. Many non-meat dishes, but succulent meats will tempt carnivores too. Good choice of local wines.

Buca San Lorenzo
Grosseto *Tel: 0564 25142*
Also in an alcove of the city walls but a larger, more elegant place. Choice of fish or meat dishes or tasting menus at different prices.

San Giorgio
Grosseto *Tel: 0564 20168*
Good for a quick, light meal, even pizza (evenings only). Choice of pastas, sauces and of fried and roast meats.

Above *Land in the Maremma is intensely cultivated, mostly with grain. Olives, the next most important crop, cluster on the hills.*

ahead at over 1700m. The hilltop town to the left is Montegiovi, then some outcrops of bare, blue-grey clay mark the arrival at Arcidosso. Take a large U-turn to the right at the town's entrance, towards Monticello. The scenery changes extremely quickly. Past Monticello, the country opens out into what looks like a rather rougher version of Montalcino. This is Cinigiano, with small producers making wines shadowing those of Montalcino. Fifteen minutes later you cross the River Ombrone. At the next junction turn left for the road to Grosseto.

GROSSETO

Grosseto is a self-assured, small smart town. It's convenient for shopping since you can find everything within a small radius. It was once a walled city, dominated by its Medici fortress. The ramparts of the city walls have been preserved and are now a broad walkway. Much of the old moat has been left, grassed, apart from some sections used as car parks. (The centre, like most Italian towns, is pedestrianised.) Life, as usual, centres round the main piazza where there is a cathedral and the ornate Palazzo della Provincia.

THE MAREMMA

The name Maremma most probably derives from *marittima*, land by the sea. It is synonymous with Grosseto province, but in fact has different boundaries including a little territory in the adjacent province of Viterbo (in Lazio, not Tuscany). It is noticeably warmer than northern Tuscany, the light more golden, the air balmier. If you like bright light, open spaces, softly undulating hills cutting across azure skies, frequent glimpses of the sea and innumerable extensive views with olive trees dominating the landscape, you'll like the Maremma.

Although hills are never far away, there is a broadish strip of coastal plain. This is perfectly flat and was, until a massive programme of drainage in the 1930s, marshland. A fast road and railway line now run through it. The road is the Aurelia, the SS1, the first state road (from Rome to the French border), built by Mussolini as part of his plans to give Italy a modern road network. Today's new Aurelia runs parallel in parts to the old Aurelia, which itself is a reworking of the original Roman Aurelia. The name, however, remains.

The local long-horned cattle are the Maremmana breed. It is a matter of great local pride that they have longer horns than the Chianina. The Maremma also houses one of Italy's most important natural parks, along the coast north and south of Alberese; a bird sanctuary on Orbetello, protected by the WWF which also controls a nature reserve at Burano.

ENOTECHE/FOOD SHOPPING

All you need to do is find Via San Martino, running behind the Palazzo della Provincia off the main piazza. There are several food shops: a *gastronomia*, a butcher, an *enoteca* and more. There is another a good butcher, Leo Chiti, in Via dei Barberi, selling prepared meat products as well as the more traditional cuts.

Above *Grosseto is a clean, well cared for place where modern development has not been allowed to ruin the old centre.*

Below *Maremma's coastal plain was once overrun by mosquitos in summer and can be fiercely humid.*

Morellino di Scansano

MORELLINI DI SCANSANO

RECOMMENDED PRODUCERS

Erik Banti
Tel: 0564 602956
Banti is an exuberant protagonist for Morellino. His richly rounded wines have great personality. Also a restaurateur, Banti makes Morellino crus Aquilaia and Ciabatta and a red from the Alicante grape.

Bargagli
Tel: 0564 599237
An up-and-coming estate; much cited.

Mantellassi
Tel: 0564 592037
The oldest Morellino estate (since 1958). Giuseppe Mantellassi runs everything with the personal touch, even deliveries. Firm, chunky, stylish wines. Wide range produced, including four types of Morellino di Scansano.

Le Pupille
Tel: 0564 505129
The biggest, punchiest and, most agree, the classiest wines of the area. They owe much to the use of *barrique* and to the efforts of super-consultant, Giacomo Tachis. Morellino Riserva is the flagship, Saffredi (Cabernet Sauvignon, with Merlot and Alicante) the attention grabber.

RESTAURANTS

Da Sandra
Magliano *Tel: 0564 592196*
Rich, wholesome, local fare; too tasty for self-restraint. Fair choice of local wines. Closed Mondays.

Right *The Cantina Sociale di Morellino is one of Europe's highest cellars (at 600m).*

Morellino di Scansano, southern Tuscany's most important wine, was originally made by people taking refuge in its high hills to escape the Maremma swamps in summer. The wine was recently highly fashionable in Florence, yet it remains poorly known in the UK.

THE WINE

The wine is made from at least 85 percent Sangiovese, here called Morellino. Some producers use exclusively Sangiovese, others add the following grape varieties: Canaiolo, Ciliegiolo, Malvasia Nera or, most often, Alicante. Alicante's origins are in Spain (where it is called Garnacha). This variety is also grown in southern France (Grenache) and Sardinia (Cannonau). Those who use it say it is responsible for Morellino's characteristic flavour: Chianti-like but with a softer, lighter yet richer and more open style. Others attribute this to the warmer climate of the area and the lighter soil. Most pride is invested in the Riserva wines which are given two years' ageing, at least one of which is spent in cask. The word Morellino is a diminutive of morello. This could refer to the wine's colour, or to the breed of horses, *cavalli morelli*, that once drew the carriages of Grosseto's aristocracy.

THE VINEYARDS

The area is extensive, forming a diamond shape from just east of Grosseto to the Termedi Saturnia in the west, and equivalent distances north–south. To see it at its best approach from the south. From Grosseto, follow the Aurelia to Albinia. This first stretch gives a good impression of the Maremma's extensive plain, with hills off to the left, cloaked in olive trees and Mediterranean scrub.

The Albinia turn-off leads into an area of mixed cultivation: sugar beet, melon and other fruits and vegetables such as aubergine, onion and tomato. A couple of minutes further on, past the level crossing, fork left (signed to Magliano and Scansano). For a while you continue through the Maremma plains, then the road rises. Olives dominate the scenery, while here and there chestnut trees, highly prized for their medicinal purposes, line the road. The area is also dotted with the remains of numerous Etruscan settlements and it is believed that the Etruscans were the first people to plant the olive here.

Fifteen minutes' drive brings you up to Magliano, a quiet village just under 130 metres high: enough to give excellent views of Monte Argentario and the Isola del Giglio. Its 15th-century city walls are quite a sight. From here, you are properly in Morellino country. The road (signposted Pereta) continues to rise in curves and twists. Ten minutes on you pass Mantellassi with fabulous views over the Argentario. Another two minutes and you pass the vineyards of Le Pupille before reaching Pereta. From here the land gets wilder, the slopes steeper and the forest area increases. The sea view reappears just as you cross a *fosso* (deep ditch). Two bends later, there is a lay-by with stunning views out to sea, south to Parrina and into Lazio, east to Manciano and Pitigliano. Further on comes Bargagli and a huge Roman villa before you reach Scansano itself.

From Scansano, turn left to head back towards Grosseto. The descent is quicker, past Pancole and Montorgiali to the outskirts of Grosseto, which takes about two hours.

Above *The hill top town of Scansano, was once the summer seat of the Grosseto bureaucracy.*

Antica Trattoria Aurora
Magliano *Tel: 0564 592030*
Speciality cheeses used with various accompaniments and there is also wide range of *antipasti*. Long wine list including dessert wines.

Franco e Silvana
Bivio di Montorgiali
Tel: 0564 580214
Simple and unchanged for generations. Typical Maremma fare from local ingredients, rustic but good. There are also fish dishes.

Ponte Rotto
Istia Ponte (Istia d'Ombrone)
Tel: 0564 409373
Delightfully located beside the Ombrone River. Fish and sea-food complements the usual Tuscan dishes. Pan-Italian wine list. Good value.

PLACES OF INTEREST

Olivo della Strega
Magliano. The oldest known olive tree: estimates of its age vary but 'several centuries' is the general consensus.

Montorgiali
April 23. Celebration of St George. Four horse riders in Roman costume parade to St George's sanctuary.

Parrina to Pitigliano

If the weather is gloomy where you are, try whizzing down to Tuscany's southern corner for a day or two. It is often sunny there when all around is under a cloud.

A day is barely sufficient, though, to explore the southern zones of Parrina, Ansonica Costa dell' Argentario and Bianco di Pitigliano: not because the viticulture is so extensive, but because of the other attractions including the panoramic hill-top towns of Capalbio, Manciano, Pitigliano, and Sovana. However you decide to spend your time, first head down the Aurelia to Albinia. From there, continue to Quattre Strada, where you turn left to enter the zone of Parrina.

PARRINA

Parrina is a small zone with just one producer, Tenuta La Parrina. Although the area looks flat, the vineyards are a good way behind, on foothill slopes and worth visiting for the views alone. The wine comes in red, white and rosé. The red and rosé are primarily from Sangiovese (70 per-cent minimum) and the white from a blend, Trebbiano with Chardonnay and/or Ansonica.

PARRINA AND ENVIRONS

RECOMMENDED PRODUCERS

Tenuta La Parrina
Tel: 0564 862636
Ignore the description 'Vino Etrusco': this is serious stuff. The red is one of the cheeriest, fruitiest, most drinkable wines of Tuscany, while the Riserva retains the fruit but has more weight and longevity. Covers almost 430ha, 53ha of which are dedicated to vineyard; 160ha are Mediterranean scrub, the rest are used for olives, table grapes, almonds, plums, pears, potatoes, beehives, sheep (for *pecorino*), goats. *Agriturismo.*

La Stellata
Manciano
Tel: 0564 620190
A smallish estate making Lunaia, the only worthy Bianco di Pitigliano.

Rascioni e Cecconello
Fonteblanda
Just off the Aurelia. Working wonders with the scantly-regarded Ciliegiolo grape variety in Poggio Ciliegia. Also Poggio Capitana.

ENOTECHE

Rosso e Pasioni
Orbetello *Tel: 0564 868140*
More a wine bar than an *enoteca*. Aperitifs; snack meals of *bruschetta* with a wide range of tasty toppings. All Italian. Can buy bottles too. No credit cards. Closed Wednesdays.

HOTELS

There are resort hotels along the coast. Otherwise most rooms, and *agriturismi*, are near Saturnia.

Albergo La Stellata
Località Pian del Bagno, Saturnia
Tel: 0564 602934
Owned by Terme di Saturnia, but

ANSONICA COSTA DELL'ARGENTARIO

This is a new DOC, although wine from the white Ansonica grape has been made in the area for years. The puzzle is how the grape arrived, for Ansonica (also written Ansonaca, Ansonaco, Anzonica) is a Sicilian grape, there called Inzolia, but found nowhere else on the peninsula. It is reckoned that that 18th-century Sicilians, disturbed by Spanish invasions, took flight taking the vine with them. Some landed on Isola del Giglio, the small island west of Monte Argentario where production is still concentrated, before proceeding to the mainland. Ansonica, though susceptible to disease, thrived on the stony, limestone soil.

Intriguing as its origins may be, few of the vines are enthralling. Most producers stick rigidly to making 'traditional' styles, which are dark-coloured, hefty, a touch tannic from skin maceration and well oxidised. Some are quite drinkable, given the right circumstances, but not exactly worth seeking out. Practically the only decent modern-style Ansonica is from Cantina Sociale di Capalbio; even there the future is uncertain as their technical director left in 1995.

Nevertheless, the production zone is a must, for its unique and beautiful geography. Monte Argentario is a large lump of forested land attached to the mainland by three causeways, creating two lagoons, both bird sanctuaries. The

aiming to create a more typically Tuscan, country house environment. Five minutes from spa.

Acquaviva
Montemerano *Tel: 0564 602890*
Quiet, friendly place on Scansano road. Comfortable, simple, well furnished rooms. Also a wine estate.

Terme di Saturnia See page 107.

RESTAURANTS

Bacco in Toscana Porto Ercole
Tel: 0564 833078. One of the best Argentario fish restaurants.

Orlando Porto Santo Stefano
Tel: 0564 814885. Fish-based menu. Good for a leisurely meal. Good wine list. Fabulous views from a large terrace.

Far left *Parrina: worth visiting if only for the views. On a clear day Elba and even Corsica can be seen.* Below and bottom *The Isola del Giglio is the nucleus of Ansonica production. Ferries sail from Porto Santo Stefano.*

La Capanna Via Aurelia *Tel: 0564 890145.* Simple dishes but they must be good, the lorry drivers eat here! Try the *acquacotta* or the wild boar.
Da Paolino Manciano *Tel: 0564 629388.* Long-standing local landmark. Good wholesome local dishes.
Passaparola Montemerano *Tel: 0564 602827.* A traditional *trattoria*. Good local food. Decent choice of wines. Excellent value.
Da Caino Montemerano *Tel: 0564 602817.* One of Italy's top-notch restaurants and cellars. Worth prices.
Enoteca dell'Antico Frantoio *Tel: 0564 602615.* Erik Banti's place. Morellino, good range of top Italian wine plus his stamp of friendliness. Wide choice of traditional dishes.
Verdiana Pomonte, nr Saturnia *Tel: 0564 599184.* Excellent selection of flavoured *crostini*, soups and game. Selection of local wines.

Main picture and above *Pitigliano is built on a mass of yellow volcanic tufa, full of holes, many of which are used as cellars.* Top right *Cats are often kept as pets in Italy, but many fend for themselves, as here, in Pitigliano.* Right *Abundant Tuscan herbs.*

outer causeways also have beaches, the middle one houses the traffic-clogged town of Orbetello.

From the Parrina road continue to the next major junction and turn left towards Albinia. There cross the Aurelia and take the northerly causeway, Tombolo della Giannella, to Porto Santo Stefano, a well-to-do harbour town lively even in winter and jam-packed in summer; *the* place to eat fish. Continue on excitingly rough roads, right round the promontory, returning through the smaller, prettier Porto Ercole and back on the middle causeway, through Orbetello. You need a good couple of hours to do it justice.

Back on the Aurelia continue southward past Ansedonia, an Etruscan city, where atmospheric ancient Roman engineering works designed to stop the port silting up can be seen. Pass Lake Burano, another bird sanctuary, then turn left to Capalbio. Capalbio glories in its 15th-century walls, still intact, circling the town giving 360° views. From there, head north for Marsiliana, a castle perched on a wooded, conical hill. Turn right towards Manciano, leaving the Ansonica Costa dell'Argentario wine zone behind.

BIANCO DI PITIGLIANO

The Pitigliano wine area stretches across the southern corner of Tuscany with an additional spur overlapping half the Morellino area, looping around Scansano. You enter the zone shortly after Marsiliana, roughly at Sgrillozzo (by the first road to the right, leading back to Capalbio).

The best wine is grown on tufa soils and made primarily from Trebbiano with a host of other varieties sometimes included: Greco, Malvasia Bianca, Verdello, Grechetto, Riesling Italico, Sauvignon, Pinot Bianco and Chardonnay. As Trebbiano is such a neutral grape variety, styles vary considerably, as does quality.

The road to Pitigliano is varied, sporadically twisty. with no more than occasional vineyard patches but fascinating throughout. After ambling round the town, have a look at Sovana, five minutes on: another medieval village perched on a volcanic rock.

From Sovana you could return the way you came. Pitigliano, seen against a setting sun, is magnificent. Otherwise, continue roughly westward to Saturnia and from there to Montemerano, home of Erik Banti (see p102). From here you can cut back to Manciano to return to Grosseto via Albinia. Otherwise turn right at the entrance to Montemerano, towards Scansano, to see more of the Bianco di Pitigliano zone, here also part of the Morellino di Scansano area. Pass through Scansano but, for a different route back to Grosseto (see p100), fork left onto a minor road to Montiano (towards Fonteblanda) and turn right again, signposted Grosseto, just before reaching the village.

Scilla Sovana *Tel: 0564 616531*
Firm emphasis on the area's traditions, so local ingredients are used. Good range of Tuscan wines.

PLACES OF INTEREST

Terme di Saturnia
Tel: 0564 601061
Italian flair at its best has created a luxury resort around the spa of Saturnia. Super-comfortable (and suitably expensive) hotel. Try with a daily ticket (all treatments extra) or, just down the road, have a hot, sulphurous, mineral bath for free.

SPECIAL EVENTS

Palio Marinaro Porto San Stefano, 15 August. Rowing regatta with four competitors representing the districts of the town, preceded by a parade in traditional costumes.

Monteregio di Massa Marittima

MASSA MARITTIMA

RECOMMENDED PRODUCERS

Meleta
Tel: 0564 567155
Some of the area's classiest wines. Rosso della Rocca (Cabernet Sauvignon and Sangiovese), Bianco della Rocca (Chardonnay), Pietrello and Pietrello d'Oro (Sangiovese).

Il Pupillo
Tel: 0566 37230
18th-century cellars, varietal wines including Pinot Bianco, Pinot Grigio,

Most of the wines from the area north of Grosseto are clustered under the newish umbrella DOC Monteregio di Massa Marittima. It covers red, white and rosé wines, including a red Riserva; red and white Vin Santo; a vino novello; and a white made almost exclusively from Vermentino. Otherwise the whites are from Trebbiano blended with all or any of Malvasia, Ansonica, Vermentino and others; the reds and rosés mainly from Sangiovese. The area covers much of the hilly area north of the city and spreads from Roccastrada in the east almost to the coast, on mainly clay soils, rich in skeletal remains. Vineyards are dotted here and there but it is an area of mixed agriculture with the olive dominating, as it does throughout the province.

OIL, WINE AND SCENERY

From Grosseto head northward. If you take the old Aurelia, running parallel to the new Aurelia, it is a little slower but much less busy and easier for visiting places, east and west. It is certainly worth diverting, after just a few minutes, both left to Vetulonia, once one of the most important Etruscan cities, and still with a major necropolis, and right to Montepescali, an enchanting medieval hill-top village. From the road you can also see, on the right, Tuscany's biggest wine bottling plant ConViMar and OlMa, Grosseto's biggest, most modern, cold-pressing cooperative for olive oil.

Top *Relaxing in Massa Marittima.*
Above *Just by the car park at the entrance to Massa Marittima, an elegant plaque shows the layout of this medieval town.*
Right *In fine weather, the elders of southern Tuscan villages bring a chair outside to sit and watch the world go by.*

Just past Montepescali fork right to Montemassi. After five to ten minutes there is a choice. Either turn right towards Roccastrada and head upward through Mediterranean scrub and cork trees, passing Poggio Oliveto at Venturi; or turn left to Montemassi and Roccatederighi via Meleta (both a locality and an estate), then turn right to Roccastrada. At 475 metres this is a fabulous vantage point; sometimes, on a very clear day, the Montalcino vineyards to the east may be visible. Head straight back down (signposted Grosseto) and, just by Montepescali, take the right turn towards Follonica onto the old Aurelia (signposted Castiglione della Pescaia).

You could divert off towards Grilli to see *Frantoio* San Luigi. Otherwise pass the town of Gavorrano, on the left. Turn left at the second signpost for Bagno di Gavorrano and go straight towards Scarlino. (The turn-off for central Scarlino leads to a sequence of tight bends up to the village,

perched on a pine-carpeted hill and with great sea views.) Just ahead on the left is Il Pupillo. Turn right, back across the Aurelia to Cura Nova, where, just on the right, is the large estate Morisfarms. Then continue to Massa Marittima.

MASSA MARITTIMA

This terrific 10th-century village, 380 metres high and built to a careful plan, was once called Massa Metallorum and was the prosperous centre of a silver, copper and other metal mining area. It is now named 'Marittima' to distinguish it from the Massa near Carrara (see p125) and is dominated by its large, central piazza around which all the municipal and church buildings cluster. There is a spot to admire the surroundings, wander, grab a bite to eat, or simply sit and people-watch. By the side of the cathedral is a wonderful old cellar belonging to Morisfarms, carved from the friable rock of the massif. The cellar is open daily (except Wednesdays) and at the entrance there is a range of food products and ceramics, plus wines, of course, to buy.

Vernaccia. All made with care by Laura Benelli and her husband.

Morisfarms
Tel: 0566 918091
Leading producer in the area and worth a visit if only for the superb views from the estate's terrace.

OLIVE OIL PRODUCERS

Poggio Oliveto Valeria Cittadini is fanatical about olive oil. No effort is spared, no detail ignored to make sure it is in perfect condition. The *frantoio* is strictly traditional, nothing that might make life easier but could compromise quality is countenanced. All is explained in as much detail as you need. The oil is splendid.

Frantoio San Luigi New cold-pressing olive oil plant but traditional granite wheels and vertical presses are used. Well set up for visitors. Snacks and meals can be provided.

RESTAURANTS

Da Nada Roccatederighi *Tel: 0564 567226*. Rustic but well flavoured traditional dishes. Also a good chance to try Meleta wines.

Vecchia Hosteria Gavorranno *Tel: 0566 844980*. *Trattoria* with local dishes and a reasonable selection of Tuscan wines. Good value.

Balbo Scarlino *Tel: 0566 37204* Large, bustling place, popular with the locals. Decent range of wines.

San Leopoldo Follonica *Tel: 0566 40645*. Light but flavoursome dishes across the whole gamut of fish and seafood. Average wines.

Santarino Follonica *Tel: 0566 41665* Fish-based *trattoria* on the busiest part of the coast, a favourite with locals. Straightforward house wine.

Bracali Massa Marittima, località Ghirlanda *Tel: 0566 902318*. The area's smartest place. Traditional basis but individual touches and thoughtful blends of flavours. Wide choice of dishes and wines. Good cheeses.

Da Tronca Massa Marittima *Tel: 0566 901991*. Friendly place. Some local dishes, some not. Great wine choice. Inexpensive.

COASTAL RESORTS

Castiglione della Pescaia is a fishing port with long, fine, sandy beach and medieval village above.

Punta Ala has superb beach and resort facilities.

Cala Violino is a quiet bay.

Follonica is a major resort with a glorious white sand beach.

Val di Cornia

VAL DI CORNIA

RECOMMENDED PRODUCERS

Iacopo Banti Campiglia Marittima *Tel: 0565 838802*
Five kilometres from the sea, overlooking Populonia and Elba and with vineyards at 250–300m, this is one of the Val di Cornia's best-sited estates and the emphasis is on quality and style. There are also large olive groves, own *frantoio*, a lemon-flavoured oil and grappa.

Gualdo del Re Suvereto, località Notri. *Tel: 0565 829888*
Small estate owned by the Rossi family. The vines are tightly pruned and quite densely planted and the cellars recently renovated . Wines have intriguing aromas and well balanced fruit. Also produce Vigna Valentina (Vermentino), a Pinot Bianco and 'Gualdo del Re' (*barrique*-matured Sangiovese). Also olive oil, grappa.

Tua Rita Suvereto, località Notri *Tel: 0565 49471*
Small estate recently founded by a pair of enthusiasts, aided by a young, bright consultant winemaker and wines already making waves. Tightly pruned, densely planted, low vines

Most of the Val di Cornia's estates are clustered around its centre, Suvereto. Many vines grow on the lowest, gentlest slopes within a stone's throw of the distinctly unpicturesque broad Cornia Valley, which is crossed by several tributaries as well as the River Cornia itself. However, sea breezes blowing along the valley ventilate the vineyards and temper the climate; most vines are low-trained and tightly pruned, many enjoying higher slopes further from the river, so prospects for good wines are better than they appear.

The reds, like most in Tuscany, are predominantly from Sangiovese and there is also a Riserva. Optionally, one or more of Canaiolo, Ciliegiolo, Cabernet Sauvignon or Merlot can be added. The whites, as usual, are based on Trebbiano Toscano. Sometimes 15–30 percent of Vermentino is added, but usually less. Other varieties which may be used include Pinot Bianco, Pinot Grigio, Clairette and the local Biancone (found also on Elba and Corsica) as well as the more normal Malvasia and Ansonica. Some producers also make a rosé (from Sangiovese).

You could rush straight up to the area on the Aurelia before cutting inland. However if your last port of call was Massa Marittima (see p109) there is a wonderful cut-through across diverse terrain. Head down from Massa Marittima following signs towards Siena. At the bottom, there appears to be a choice between two almost parallel

Above *Not just a relaxing shady spot, but a chance to discuss the important matters in life.*
Right *The Val di Cornia valley.*

Above right *The Val di Cornia combines vine, olive and wheat.*
Below right *Summer in Elba, all types of tomatoes for sale.*

roads straight ahead. But there is a garage on the left, and just to the side of it a tiny, single-track road which requires almost a U-turn to get onto it. As you do, a small, almost illegible yellow sign confirms that this is the way to Suvereto. Apart from intensively cultivated small plots of mixed crops and wooded slopes you will see numerous large, healthy cork trees. The road leads through Montebamboli and a series of curves. Once it straightens out there is a crossroads. Go straight ahead to San Lorenzo, where there is the greatest concentration of vineyards, low, neat and tidy, since leaving Montalcino. A road of sorts cuts across from here to Suvereto, but it is difficult to find, and is actually little more than a rutted track going straight through a couple of the Cornia's tributaries (which could easily be dried up

give concentrated, rich wines. Giusto di Notri (Cabernet and Merlot), Perlato del Bosco (Sangiovese, old vines from excellent site, also a white version), Sileno (Riesling, Chardonnay and Traminer). Also olive oil, grappa.

Bulichella Suvereto, località Bulichella. *Tel: 0565 829892*
Organic produce, including oil, fruit, vegetables, cereals, honey, jams. All available from shop 'Il Bucchero' in Via Magenta, Suvereto, where there is a small tasting-room. *Agriturismo*. Meals.

Ambrosini Suvereto, località Tabarò *Tel: 0565 829301*
The Val di Cornia's only experimental vineyard. Riflesso Antico Rosso, from the Montepulciano grape of Abruzzo (eastern Italy, no connection with the Tuscan town). Otherwise, two lines, both red and white: Ambrosini and Tabarò, lighter styled. Also olive oil and grappa.

ELBA

RECOMMENDED PRODUCERS

Acquabona Portoferraio, località Acquabona. *Tel: 0565 933013*
Elba's leading estate, traditional, but qualitatively minded. Wide range of varieties grown. Good wines, particularly Aleatico.

La Chiusa Portoferraio, località Magazzini. *Tel: 0565 933046*
Vineyards on hills overlooking the sea. Concentration on sweet and *passito* wines, notably Aleatico.

HOTELS

Most are by the coast. Many are closed in winter and booked solid in summer, so, unless travelling out of season, plan ahead. Otherwise, you could stay in Volterra. Several estates in the Val di Cornia offer *agriturismo*.

Right *Portoferraio, Elba.*
Below A *calm moment in the fish market in Castiglione della Pescaia.*
Far right *Not often do palm trees punctuate a vineyard, as in Elba.*
Below right *Despite Piombino's ugliness, there are beautiful corners.*

RESTAURANTS

Enoteca Pizzica
Campiglia Marittima. *Tel: 0565 838383*
Despite the name, this is a proper restaurant. Varied dishes based loosely on local styles. Selection of Tuscan wines. Panoramic terrace for eating outside.

Otello
Venturina. *Tel: 0565 851212*
Simple *trattoria*, good for quick meals. Choice of meat or fish dishes, fair wine list. Good range of Val di Cornia wines and some other Tuscans.

Summertime
Elba, Capoliveri *Tel: 0565 935180*
Owners have lived in New York, hence unusual name. Mainly fish and better choice and atmosphere in summer. Good selection of wines, but oddly, mostly red.

Le Palme
Elba, Bagnaia di Portoferraio
Tel: 0565 961096. Locally caught fish bursting with flavour. All served in attractive garden. Good value.

Da Luciano
Elba, Portoferraio, località Scaglieri della Biodola. *Tel: 0565 969952*
More than decent restaurant with huge terrace overlooking the sea. Fish- based.

Rendez Vous
Elba, Marciana Marina. *Tel: 0565 99251.* Long-standing reputation. Typical Elban cuisine. Good for eating outside. Good wine list.

in summer) so it is probably best to turn back. Once back at the cross-roads, fork left towards Suvereto, passing through another intensely cultivated patch of vineyard before the road begins to climb into the town itself.

Suvereto's streets curve round the hillside forming a set of concentric half-circles crossed by steep cut-throughs. Romanesque and medieval buildings combine with marble-fronted buildings, making it unusually attractive. Don't be fooled by the signs to 'Belvedere', though. They lead to a hamlet ten minutes above Suvereto (– not a lay-by with a great panorama). From Suvereto either cut straight through to the Bolgheri area (see p114) on a tiny twisting road signposted to Sassetta, or zoom down past Campiglia Marittima and Venturina towards the coastal town of Piombino.

PIOMBINO

Piombino is an eyesore. It is a heavily industrial area with metal smelters pumping out fumes and polluting the atmosphere, although it does have a reasonably well preserved centre. Unfortunately, if you want to take a ferry across to the island of Elba, you have to fight through Piombino's traffic and its fumes (unless you sail from Livorno, much further north). You also need to get within sniffing distance of it to visit the Etruscan miracle of Populonia.

If signs to this ancient site prove elusive, follow those for San Vincenzo until a left turn to Populonia is signposted.

Within a couple of minutes you pass a major necropolis, with tombs from all periods and of all types. The custodian (who speaks no English, unfortunately) will open the area for you on request. The road skates along the coast, rising through woods. Look carefully and you will see an ancient head carved into the rock.

Etruscan Populonia was – as the town of Piombino is today – a centre of ore extraction. Its most significant structure now is the peaceful, squat, round-turreted Medici castle. Populonia's coastline is a confirmed beauty-spot.

ELBA

Elba is best visited out of season. The thousands of tourists' and holidaymakers' cars going across to the island in summer can turn its panoramic narrow twisting roads into gridlocked frustration.

The island is rich in mineral reserves. Many are ferrous compounds or semi-precious stones, so for something more active than sunbathing (most beaches are rocky, a few pebbly or sandy) try a treasure hunt.

The wines, reputedly, also have a mineral tang. It is not pronounced, however, as most are made light and easy to satisfy the thirsts of the many holiday-makers, who drink practically all the production. The reds are mainly Sangiovese, the whites based on Trebbiano, although there is also some white Ansonica (also a sweet *passito* version), a little Vin Santo, some sparkling wine and a sweet red made from the Aleatico variety.

Publius
Elba, Poggio di Marciana.
Tel: 0565 99208
It seems a shame to be on Elba and not eat by the coast but if you want Elba's best wine list, this is the place to come. Choice of excellently cooked fish or meat dishes. Good value.

FOOD SHOPPING

Covered market
Via delle Galeazze, Portoferraio. Well worth a browse around, especially for the fish.

Bolgheri

THE WINES

Just the thought of the Bogheri area is enough to bring a frisson of excitement to Italian wine enthusiasts. The idea of seeing the home of Sassicaia, the estate which almost single-handedly convinced a doubting world that Italy could produce top-class wines, draws folk from all around. But don't get too keyed up. Sassicaia and its rival, the almost equally famous Ornellaia, are two of the few estates in Italy which do not encourage visitors – it is not even worth trying.

Strangely, the Bolgheri area does not look or feel much like a wine zone. Most is practically flat and very close to the sea, although hills do rise up behind. The soil is mainly thick clay, naturally more suited to olive or fruit trees. Vines have been planted in stonier areas where there is better drainage.

The DOC of Bolgheri was created so that renegades like Sassicaia could fit into the system. Its controls are stricter than most with regard to yields, but much looser on grape varieties. Bolgheri Rosso can contain up to 70 percent Sangiovese, 70 percent Merlot or 80 percent Cabernet Sauvignon allowing a wide variation of styles – a trend that some would like to see other areas following. Bolgheri Bianco, from Trebbiano, Vermentino or Sauvignon, has similar freedom in varietal make-up. There are also single

Right *Sassicaia's cellars are at the end of the 5km-long Strada di Cipressi. This cypress-lined avenue, planted in 1801, was immortalised by Carducci in a poem familiar to every Italian school child.*

Below *The grapes of Bolgheri are subject to tight controls over the weight of crop per hectare, number of vines per hectare, weight of crop per vine and volume of juice.*

Bolgheri

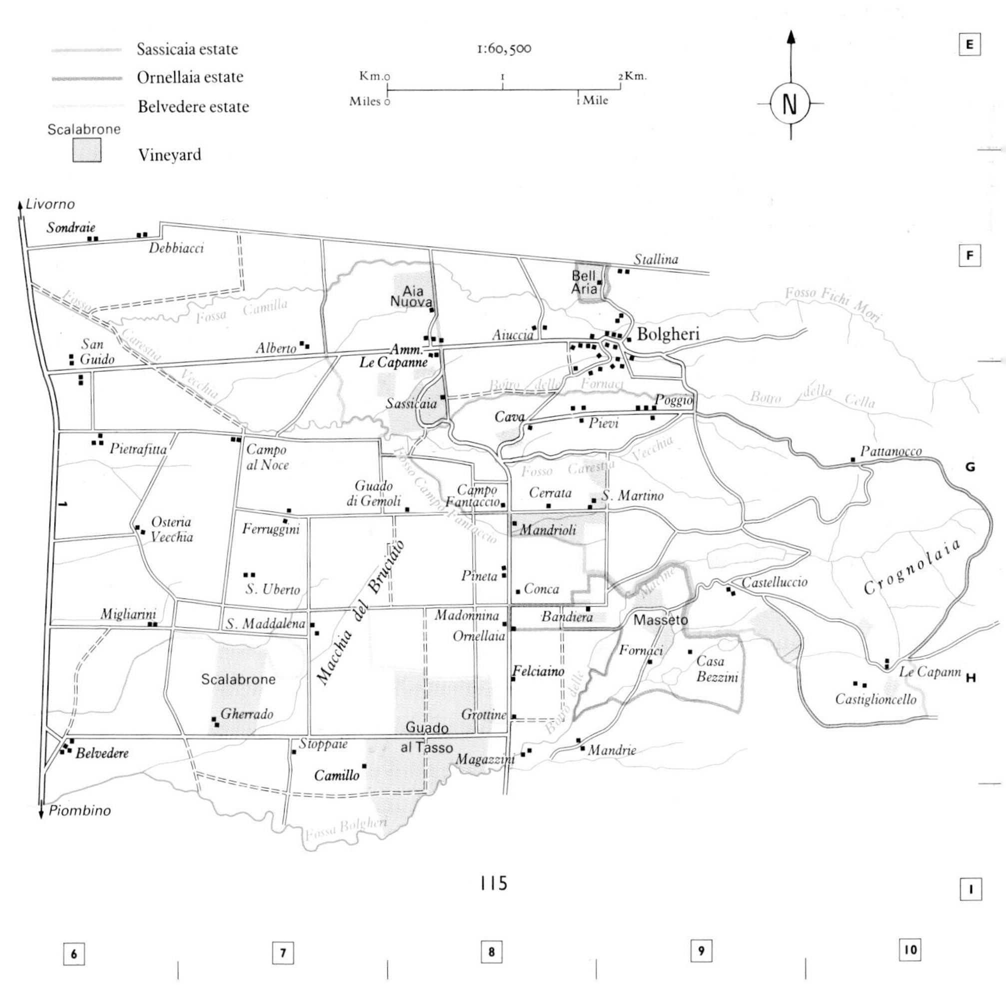
Sassicaia estate
Ornellaia estate
Belvedere estate
Scalabrone
Vineyard
1:60,500
Km.0
1
2 Km.
Miles 0
1 Mile
N
Livorno
Sondraie
Debbiacci
Fossa Camilla
San Guido
Alberto
Aia Nuova
Amm.
Le Capanne
Sassicaia
Aiuccia
Bell Aria
Stallina
Bolgheri
Fosso Fichi Mori
Botro delle Fornaci
Botro della Cella
Cava
Pievi
Poggio
Pietrafitta
Campo al Noce
Guado di Gemoli
Campo Fantaccio
Cerrata
S. Martino
Pattanocco
Osteria Vecchia
Ferruggini
Mandrioli
S. Uberto
Pineta
Conca
Castelluccio
Crognolaia
Migliarini
S. Maddalena
Macchia del Bruciato
Madonnina
Ornellaia
Bandiera
Masseto
Fornaci
Casa Bezzini
Scalabrone
Felciaino
Le Capanne
Castiglioncello
Gherrado
Grottine
Guado al Tasso
Belvedere
Stoppaie
Camillo
Magazzini
Mandrie
Piombino
Fossa Bolgheri

Right *The medieval village of Bolgheri.*
Far right *A vineyard worker carefully tends the strictly controlled vineyards of Bolgheri.*

BOLGHERI

RECOMMENDED PRODUCERS

Sassicaia
(Officially **'Tenuta San Guido'**) Mostly Cabernet Sauvignon, the vines were brought from Château Lafite in the 1940s and the wines, which some reckon to be Italy's finest, are massive and extremely long-lived. Priced accordingly.

Tenuta dell'Ornellaia Mostly from Cabernet Sauvignon, with Merlot and Cabernet Franc. Huge Masseto (Merlot) and whites receive rapturous praise.

Grattamacco
Tel: 0565 763840. Not quite in the league of Sassicaia and Ornellaia but more approachable, more drinkable – more affordable. Also more accommodating. Olive oil too.

Tentua Belvedere
Tel: 0565 749735. Another large estate owned by Piero Antinori. The Cabernet flagship is Gaudo al Tasso, which is almost in Sassicaia class.

Le Macchiole
Tel: 0565 777725. Owning land a stone's throw from the top vineyards of Bolgheri, Eugenio Campolmi could not resist trying his hand at winemaking. Best Cabernet wine is Paleo Rosso.

Michele Satta
Tel: 0565 763483. An estate standing by Sangiovese, eg Vigna del Cavaliere.

RESTAURANTS

Gambero Rosso
San Vincenzo *Tel: 0565 701021*
An unimposing entrance but one of Italy's top restaurants. It is known for its purée of chickpeas with prawns; fish-stuffed black ravioli; roast pigeon with the legs (fried) in a salad; crème brûlée. New dishes always emerging. Superb wine list. Not cheap, but neither should it be. Must book.

Il Bambolo
Castegneto Carducci *Tel: 0565 775055*
Enjoyed by locals. Choice of meat or fish menus: solid, reliable. Fair wine list.

Da Ugo
Castegneto Carducci *Tel: 0565 763746*
Long-standing, congenial restaurant. Strictly traditional fare augmented by fish in summer. Order some vegetables with the main course to drench with the excellent local olive oil. Decent wine list, local and Tuscan. Good value.

varietal versions from Vermentino and Sauvignon, red Vin Santo (called Occhio di Pernice) and a rosé. Sassicaia is now classified as an official Bolgheri sub-zone requiring at least 80 percent Cabernet Sauvignon.

THE VINEYARDS

From Populonia, head north along the coast to San Vincenzo, a sizeable resort with a long but fairly narrow beach. From there take the Aurelia (old or new) to Donoratico. In summer this stretch is packed, so leave plenty of time for what in winter is a 20-minute hop. Follow signs for Castagne to Carducci, then for Bolgheri. As soon as you leave the Aurelia you are in the Bolgheri zone and almost immediately pass the estate of Michele Satta. Turn left towards Bolgheri. Up to the right are the vineyards of the highly regarded Grattamacco. A little further on to the left, 100–200 metres from the road, is the Guado del Tasso vineyard of Piero Antinori's Tenuta Belvedere. Drive slowly and keep a watch to the right: after about five minutes the smart entrance to Ornellaia appears, a long, imposing drive behind firmly locked gates. Opposite is Le Macchiole,

Right *In some ways Bolgheri resembles Bordeaux – indeed Marchese Niccolò della Rochetta of Sassicaia created the wine partly out of his admiration for the fine Bordeaux châteaux.*

signposted Contessine. A little past Ornellaia is a tidy vineyard with very low, tightly pruned, vines. This belongs to Sassicaia – it is not marked in any way, though many less illustrious estates along the route are. The previously straight road then begins to wind: where it straightens again there is another Sassicaia vineyard to the left.

The road then crosses another which runs from the sea to Bolgheri village. Its entirety, five kilometres, is lined with cypress trees. Divert left onto this avenue to see Sassicaia's cellars, an unmarked, large pink shed on the left, just before approaching the Aurelia. Turn back, branching left to Bibbona just before reaching the medieval Bolgheri village. More Sassicaia vines are about 300 metres along on the left. Continue to medieval Bibbona, worth exploring on foot, and Casale Marittima, bringing you to the Montescudaio zone.

Da Zi' Martino
Castegneto Carducci, località San Giusto *Tel: 0565 763666*
Popular local *trattoria*. Standard menu includes soups, rabbit and chips; good plain food, excellently cooked, cheap.

ENOTECHE

San Vincenzo
Across from Gambero Rosso (see above). Superb wines with a few nibbles at terrifically good prices.

Enoteca Alimentari Tognoni
Bolgheri. Snacks: vegetable soup, *salumi*, etc, to go with Bolgheri or Chianti wines. Both Bolgheri and Castagneto Carducci have wine shops stocking many Bolgheri wines.

MONTESCUDAIO AND VOLTERRA

RECOMMENDED PRODUCERS

Fattoria Sorbaiano
Tel: 0588 30243
An individual microclimate: warm days and cool nights. Montescudaio Rosso and Bianco are both fruity and very drinkable, white Lucestraia and Rosso delle Miniere are more intense and complex. Also olive oil. *Agriturismo.*

Poggio Gagliardo
Tel: 0586 630661
Near Cecina, just east of superstrada. One of area's largest estates; complex, aromatic red and white wines of fine structure, balance and roundness.

Montescudaio and Volterra

MONTESCUDAIO

The Montescudaio vineyards cluster along the Cecina River and around the villages of Casale Marittima, Guardistallo and Montescudaio. The best way to get a feel of the area is to travel through them in turn then head down through the hills, west towards Cecina. From Cecina (which has a confusing one-way system) follow signs to Volterra, which brings you back eastwards, this time by the river. The route is punctuated with fabulous views across valleys: medieval villages, the river snaking into the distance, graceful curves, wild plunges of land, vineyards stamped across the slopes.

The red wines, as usual, are based on Sangiovese, the whites Trebbiano; the reds follow the old Chianti format adding white grapes to give a fresh, light touch.

Coming back through the valley, there are outcrops

Left *Fresh asparagus piled high on a local market stall.*
Right, far left and below *It is almost impossible not to be captivated by Volterra. From its ancient walls there are 360° views of the surrounding countryside.*

of bare, blue-grey clay. These are the first signs of the 'moonscape' that surrounds Volterra. When you reach the turning for Guardistallo divert onto it briefly. As you rise into the hills, you will see glimpses of Volterra off to the left. Turn back for a marvellous panorama of the Cecina Valley.

Once back driving along the river, vineyards become increasingly sparse. The road crosses the river and begins to rise towards Volterra, passing Saline di Volterra, site of the old salt mines that kept the Medicis wealthy.

VOLTERRA

Volterra, perched at almost 550 metres, has 3,000 years of history. It was the Etruscan capital, then a Roman town (the amphitheatre and baths still survive). Huge stretches of the old city walls are still intact (you can walk right round them), as is a massive Etruscan gate, the Porta al l'Arco. Driving is thankfully not permitted in Volterra. Its well preserved, narrow streets are a walker's delight: mainly medieval but with many Etruscan and Roman relics. Alabaster mining and sculpting was important in Etruscan times, and still is. Of the three best museums, the Guarnacci has a marvellous collection of ancient alabaster urns. Volterra is also a good base for visiting Vernaccia di San Gimignano (see p74).

From Volterra, head towards Montecatini Val di Cecina. As you sweep through the beautiful steep hills you may spot plumes of what looks like smoke out to the left. These are sites of geo-thermic electricity generators harnessing the power of volcanic hot springs. After a while the road travels along the boundary of Montescudaio. Unless you want to go to Montecatini (home of Sorbaiano) follow it right towards Pontedera. Soon you will be in the hills of the Era Valley.

HOTELS

Volterra has relatively few hotels, but you could try the following:
Etruria (0588 87377) Best value.
Albergo Villa Nencini (0588 86386), a sixteenth-century house just outside the city, with a pool.
SCAP cooperative for local villas.

RESTAURANTS

Il Frantoio
Montescudaio *Tel: 0586 650381*
Well known haunt. Eat well for the price. Great wine list, especially local.
Da Badò
Volterra *Tel: 0588 86477*
Family-run *trattoria*. Limited choice but top-quality ingredients. Book.

FOOD SHOPPING

Panificio La Scalinata
Via San Sebastiano 2, Montescudaio
Traditional old bakery; original wood oven still used. Fabulous old-style bread.
Frantoio I Massi
Guardistallo, località I Massi
Cold-pressed organic olive oil.
Isiano Baroncini
Via Ricciarelli 35, Volterra. Top quality Chianina beef, raw and prepared.

SPECIAL EVENTS

Polenta Festival Guardistallo.
Second Sunday in October.
Wine Festival Montescudaio.
First Sunday in October.

PISA AND ENVIRONS

RECOMMENDED PRODUCERS

Bruno & Elyane Moos
Tel: 0587 654180. Moos spent time abroad before returning to Europe to realize his dream of making wine. Now, with his French-Canadian wife, he produces eye-opening wines. He handles different varieties with aplomb, working mostly with Sangiovese but also Viognier, the rare French grape; Syrah, Merlot, Cabernet and Malvasia Nera. Soianello is the touchstone: two-thirds Sangiovese with a pot-pourri of other red grapes, slow-ageing, muscular and refined; Fontestina is 100% Sangiovese. Tiny quantities.

Tenuta di Ghizzano
Tel: 0587 630096. Owned by the noble Venerosi Pesciolini family. Best known for gentle Sangiovese/ Cabernet blend Veneroso.

Badia di Morrona
Tel: 0587 658505. Large, excellently positioned estate. Interesting wines now emerging.

RESTAURANTS: PISA

Lo Schiaccianoci
Tel: 050 21024. Highly reputed. Most restaurants offer a choice of fish- or meat-based courses. Light, original touch. Optional fixed-price menu. Great wine list. Good value.

Sergio
Tel: 050 580580
Pisa's top place. Expensive but fairly priced for the quality.

Kostas
Tel: 050 571467. Tuscan food with southern Italian influences. Fine ingredients, well handled. Carefully selected wine list, mainly Tuscan, some Italian. Good value.

Pisa and environs

COLLINE PISANE

The Pisan Hills, or the hills of Pisa's province, form a Chianti sub-zone. The idea of a Chianti, eternally associated with eastern Tuscany, Florence and Siena, coming from the maritime republic of Pisa is too much of a contradiction for the average Italian, and Chianti Colline Pisane has been regarded as something of a joke. In addition, or maybe as a result, producers have been less than industrious, letting vineyards slip into decline or just turning out the most basic wine. Most developments in the area have been instigated by non-Tuscans who have moved in although now, some locals are getting their act together too. Even so, the top estates have almost entirely turned their backs on the handicap of the Chianti denomination, preferring to use a prominent individual name together with the more neutral Colli dell'Etruria Centrale, a newish, broad-based DOC covering roughly the whole Chianti zone.

The zone's heartland, with soils of mineral-rich, hard clay, is surprisingly unknown and, except for visitors to the spa of Casciana Terme, relatively few travellers cross it. A white wine, Bianca Pisano di San Torpé is also produced in the area.

THE VINEYARDS

Heading northward from Volterra you enter the Colline Pisane. By a cypress-topped knoll to the right, about ten minutes from the Pontendera fork, you start to see single rows of vines which traditionally demarcated fields or properties. Pass La Sterza and then a junction for Terriciola. To explore the eastern half of the area go straight ahead here across the river to the beautiful old town of Peccioli, from there, just a short if tortuous hop to Ghizzano. Otherwise, turn left to Terriciola and its more uplifting backdrop, which marks the start of the Colline Pisane's heartland.

Approaching the village you see Azienda Belvedere, soon after, there is a sudden explosion of vineyard.

Continue through the village and along the hill crest to Morrona. You pass the cellar of Badia di Morrona and just ahead there is a vantage point with views of the church and the best vineyards. Within minutes you come into Soiana, another tiny village and the home of the Pisan Hills' best estate owned by Bruno and Elyane Moos. From there, head down towards Ponsacco, branching off left to Lari. At this point it becomes clear how protected Soiana and the other central villages are from Mediterranean weather systems. You cross three hill ridges in quick succession, each dominated by once feudal estates, before feeling the coastal air behind Livorno. The twists of the first rise, the steep road to Lari, give some splendid views of terraced vineyard, with Soiana up in front and Lari, with its castle, to the right. From Lari the road plunges, then rises to Crespina. From there is another swift descent and ascent to Fauglia, passing the estate Uccelliera, whose cellars are

Far left, left and below *Even when coastal Tuscany is throbbing, the Pisan hills retain their tranquility.*

La Grotta
Tel: 050 578105 Designed like a grotto. Good wine-list; lesser-known-estate selection. Snacks served late.

Osteria dei Cavalieri
Tel: 050 580858. Easy-going, friendly, modern-looking. Wide choice of single-course meals. Good wine selection.

Numero Undici
Pretend to be a Pisan and have a crêpe or a vegetable tart, some salami or lasagne in the old market. Cheap, cheerful, surprisingly good. No 'phone.

La Mescita
Near Piazza delle Vettovaglie. Much use of vegetables and herbs. Good sheep and goat cheeses. Many wines.

Il Montemagno
Montemagno Calci, 12km east of Pisa. *Tel: 050 936245*

If you are hungry and on a budget it is worth the trip. Fresh, wholesome menu changes regularly.

RESTAURANTS: LIVORNO

La Chiave
Tel: 0576 888609
Quiet, super-smart restaurant. Excellent fresh fish cooked with flair. Good wine selection. Costly.

Cantina Nardi
Tel: 0586 808006
Anything from a quick snack to a full meal. Browse for your wine. Only open at lunchtime but serving through to aperitifs time. Inexpensive.

along the valley floor road. On the way up you also pass Scopicci. After Fauglia cut down to Accaiolo and across to Torretta. You could then go straight to Livorno or delay the agony by diverting southward to Rosignano Marittima then cutting across to take the thrilling coast road back up. Unlike the sybaritic sandy beaches of further south, the upper Livorno coast is stark and rocky. The little promontory of Castiglioncello in particular is good for a stroll, wind-blown or sun-drenched.

LIVORNO

Livorno is a huge port and the usual harbour-side decay has permeated various parts of the city, making the attractive parts small oases between urban sprawl and marine seediness. The compensation is for shoppers, with better choice and prices than in Pisa. The pivotal sights are the Fortezza Vecchia and the Fortezza Nuova. The latter, built in 1590, is now dedicated to leisure, the canals surrounding it are not.

PISA

Pisa is just 15 minutes' drive north of Livorno. The approaches may be dreary, the signposting erratic, the atmosphere self-satisfied and smug, but the focal point, the Piazza del Duomo or Piazza dei Miracoli, which attracts millions of tourists and billions of Lire, is miraculous indeed. However many photographs you have seen, however many times you

Above *Weights have been loaded onto the ground to one side of the tower in an attempt to straighten it.* Left and far left (bottom) *The port of Livorno is important commercially, but the Livornese escape the grind by going to nearby resorts Ardenza and Argignano.* Far left (top) *Palazzo dei Cavalieri, Pisa.*

have visited, however many tourists are cluttering the pathways, the Leaning Tower and its adjacent cathedral and baptistery stop you in your tracks. You even forget the ranks of tacky stalls selling identical tourist gear around the place.

It is probably just as well that visitors are no longer allowed to climb the tower. Emerging from the narrow, sloping, slippery spiral staircase, onto a slanting arcaded ledge, with nothing between you and the ground is an unsettling experience.

The Arno sweeps gracefully through the city, the smart buildings on either side providing a sheltered atmosphere. The piazzas are terrific, the churches majestic; shopping is good but expensive and the centre is compact, lively and relaxed. Pisa is not at all bad.

Enoteca DOC
Tel: 0586 887583
Huge range of wines from every corner of Tuscany and all over the world. Menu from *bruschetta* and salads to the four-course works.

Il Tartufo
Tel: 0586 884735
Truffles are, logically, used wherever possible, mostly with pasta and gnocchi. Substantial portions.

FOOD SHOPPING

Central market Livorno
Scali Sassi. Great variety and abundance.

Market: Piazza delle Vettovaglie Pisa
Go for the fruit and vegetables but also meats, fish, *salumi*, breads, cheese.

Pasticceria Salza Pisa
Borgo Stretto 44/46. Renowned pastries and sweetmeats. Great ice creams. Also serves a light lunch.

Gastronomia Simi
Gastronomia Gratin Pisa
Via San Martino 6 and Via Crispi 66 respectively. Both excellent delicatessen with good quality ready-to-eat dishes, some special to Pisa.

Co-op sales point Mortellini
Via Aurelia Sud 7 (near Pisa Sud motorway exit). Good quality cheeses, meats, cooked meats, honey and more. Most also can be eaten in the adjacent restaurant (Re di Puglia).

Da Cecco and
La Torteria Gagarin
Via Cavalletti and Via del Cardinale respectively.
The places to go for *farinata*, also called *cecina*, a bread made from chick-pea flour, a Livorno speciality.

North of Pisa

MASSA-CARRARA

RESTAURANTS: CARRARA

More a place for good *trattorie* than for smart restaurants.

Gargantou
At Avenza, 4km from town centre. Family-run, simple and welcoming. Traditional local dishes. No 'phone.

L'Enoteca
Tel: 0585 634420
Ground floor houses bar, enoteca and tables for lunch; downstairs, smarter, is for dinners. Fascinating wine list.

RESTAURANTS: MASSA

Cybo
Tel: 0585 830703. In the evening, an enoteca with tutored tastings. Try tasting menu - different wines with each course. No credit cards.

Osteria del Borgo
Tel: 0585 810680 Typical, local dishes. Pan-Italian wine list – owner a wine enthusiast.

From Pisa head north towards the coast and the riviera. towards the resort towns Viareggio and smart Forte dei Marmi, the best known, which almost run into each other. The wide sandy beach is neatly carved into separate areas owned by hotels or municipalities, each with its own style and colour of changing cabins, umbrellas and loungers. Hotel beaches are for guests only; to enjoy the council beaches you pay by the day or half day for access and extra for facilities. There are odd stretches of 'public' beach, unadorned but free, but you'll need to search hard (try Lido di Camaiore). Out of season it all looks quite jolly. In season it is a seething mass of hedonistic sun-worshippers, cars and motorbikes.

The main reason for subjecting yourselves to this strip of the region is to visit the wine areas of Candia dei Colli Apuani and Colli di Luni. Trundle along the coast road until you tire of resort-land then cut inland on any of the larger roads to the Aurelia. Just north of Forte dei Marmi the province of Massa begins and, officially, the small Candia dei Colli Apuani zone, covering the hills to your right, called the Alpi Apuane. The wines are white, made principally from Vermentino, with 10–20 percent of the local grape

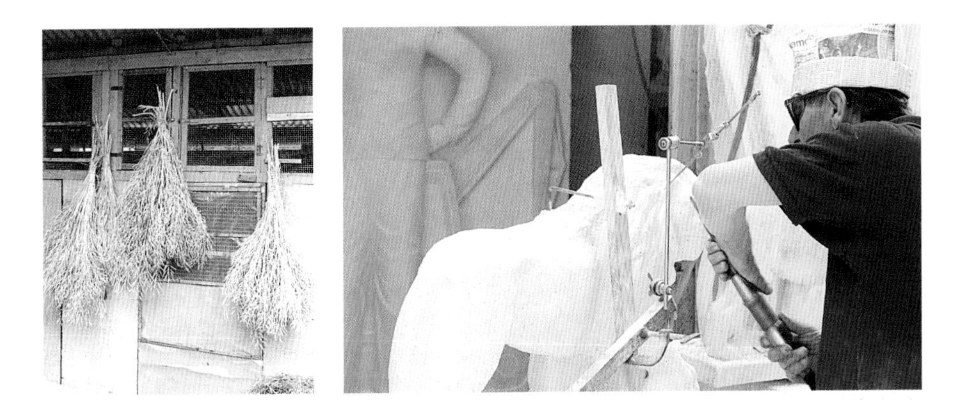

Albarola. There are only about 20 hectares of vineyard in total. Before Massa itself there are few vineyards; the view is dominated by the castle of the Malaspina, a powerful family who gained wealth by collecting tolls from the merchants and pilgrims who used this once important trade route. Just past Massa the hills are suddenly carpeted with strips and patches of vines. After a short stretch the vines disappear suddenly to be replaced by the quarried marble slopes of Carrara.

Above *The abundance of marble around Carrara is almost unworldy.*
Below *Strips and patches of vine carpet the hills around Massa.*
Far left *Massa is a working town rather than a tourist attraction, but it has a fair dose of civic pride.*

Carrara is an industrial, no-nonsense sort of town, stretching from the coast to the quarries. There is no sense of commemoration of the marble connection. Perhaps being surrounded by white slopes, thundering lorries and marble dust is enough. Just past Carrara the Colli di Luni begin. Red wines are made from about two-thirds Sangiovese, whites from Vermentino, Trebbiano and others or purely Vermentino. Most of the zone is in the neighbouring coastal region of Liguria; the small Tuscan part is inland. Almost immediately you see signs to the archeological site of Luni itself on the left. This was the original Roman marble town (now in Liguria); the surrounding area is still called the Lunigiana. After about five minutes turn right (back into Tuscany) up to Fosdinovo, the centre of Tuscan Colli di Luni wine production, with only about four hectares planted. Quantities are tiny.

Fosdinovo, the northernmost part of the route, is 500 metres high, as is much of the hilly road back to Carrara. Most is forested but there are areas of terracing and even dry stone walls. The sad thing is how many vineyards have been abandoned. After about 20 minutes' descent into Carrara, a few vineyards appear (now Candia dei Colli Apuani again). The 'back road' from Carrara to Massa through the Alpi Apuane is quite hard to find (look for signs to Bergiola) but worth it for the natural beauty and to avoid the traffic. Once back in Massa, the next port of call is Lucca.

RESTAURANTS: THE COAST

There are innumerable good places. Highlights include:

L'Oca Bianca
Viareggio *Tel: 0584 388318*
Smart dining room with panoramic views out to sea. Super-refined eating. Matching, classy wine list. Costly.

La Darsena
Via Coppino 8, Viareggio *Tel: 0584 392785.* Unaffected by touristic flux. Lunchtime better; refined and expensive in the evening. Wines from Montecarlo and further afield.

ENOTECHE

Di Vino in Vino
Via Coppino 8, Viareggio. Small place packed with Italian wines, also spirits, vinegars, *salumi*, jams and preserves.

Il Puntodivino
Via Mazzini 229, Viareggio. Wine bar but with full *trattoria*-style meals.

Lucca and environs

Lucca's city walls, set behind a grassed-over moat and clutches of chestnut trees, still circle the town. Low, thick and solid, they remain perfectly intact. Other ancient town walls, built taller but thinner, were knocked down during the 19th century when cities were rapidly expanding. Lucca's walls were rebuilt in the 16th century to survive attack and even town developers today have resisted dismantling them. As a result Lucca has changed very little (less even than Siena) and history oozes from every pore. Once an important Roman town, from which the neat grid of streets and the Piazza Amfiteatro remain, Lucca became the medieval capital of Tuscany before gaining its independence and operating as a city state until 1799. Its economy was based on banking and the silk trade. Now it is better known as Tuscany's foremost olive oil town.

The area inside the walls is quite small, and easy to cover by foot. There are several splendid churches but the highlight is San Michele in the centre of town on the site of the old Roman forum. If stopping to eat in Lucca forget the waistline: the cuisine involves liberal use of olive oil. Specialities are the barley-like grain, *farro* and chestnuts.

Lucca is also the ideal base for touring the zones of Colline Lucchesi and Montecarlo.

LUCCA AND ENVIRONS

RECOMMENDED PRODUCERS

Fattoria del Buonamico
Tel: 0583 22038
Montecarlo's most cited estate: Rosso di Cercatoio and fat white Vasario best known. But quality variable.

Le Murelle
Tel: 0583 394487
Clean, intense, balanced Sauvignon and Chardonnay. *Agriturismo.*

Camigliano
Tel: 050 643739
Well made wines; mainly white.

Fattoria dei Maionchi
Tel: 0583 978194
Magnificent villa and garden. Eminently drinkable red. Olive oil. *Agriturismo.*

Tenuta di Valgiano
Tel: 0583 40227
Brand-new estate already with Lucca's best red: youthful Rosso di Palistorti. Enthusiastic, bright young team are revitalising the area.

MONTECARLO

Montecarlo Rosso is an unexceptional mid-weight red, chiefly from Sangiovese with any or all of Canaiolo, Ciliegiolo, Colorino, Malvasia Nera, Syrah, Cabernet and others. There is as much choice with the white to enliven the basal Trebbiano: Sémillon, Pinot Grigio, Pinot Bianco, Vermentino, Sauvignon, Roussanne may all go into the pot. Nonetheless it is rare to find these varieties' flavours expressing themselves. Producers seem keener on the high-tech, light and tight approach.

Montecarlo is a tiny Medici village set atop a conical hill, its vineyards clustered around it in a compact, fairly densely planted zone. It takes about 20 minutes to reach the area from Lucca. Take the road to Altopascio (avoiding the motorway). Just past the large supermarket on the right near Porcari fork right (signed Altopascio) then immediately swing round left to Turchetto. A right turn is signposted to Montecarlo. You pass Fattoria del Buonamico on the right. At the top of the incline there is a junction signposted right for the old centre. Turning left leads down past Fattoria Michi (on the left); follow the road to the Lucca–Montecatini road junction, which will take you back to Lucca.

HOTELS

Accommodation is short in Lucca so book ahead or stay outside town.

Universo
Tel: 0583 493678
Relaxed and comfortable

La Luna
Tel: 0583 493634

Piccolo Hotel Puccini
Tel: 0583 55421
Small, unassuming, family-run feel.

RESTAURANTS

La Buca di Sant'Antonio
Lucca *Tel: 0583 578181*. Large, bustling restaurant. Tuscan wine list.

La Mora
Lucca *Tel: 0583 406402*. Seems rustic but very smart with top-notch traditional food. Varied wine list. Expensive.

Osteria del Vecchio Palazzo
Località San Pancrazio
Tel: 0583 579131. Restaurant in beautiful vineyard setting. Unusual, refreshing dishes/snacks.

Below and left *Lucca's rooftops and a* pasticceria.
Right *Eagerly awaited each autumn are* Funghi porcini.
Below right *Discarded demi-johns.*

Top left *Vineyards criss-crossing the Colline Lucchesi.*
Above *A glorious example of art nouveau architecture on a palazzo façade in Lucca.*
Left *Enjoying ice cream at one of Lucca's* gelateria.
Right *This cheese shop also sells bread and wine.*

Buatino
Lucca *Tel: 0583 343207.* Popular inexpensive *trattoria* with simple, homely fare. Local wines.
Da Giulio
Lucca *Tel: 0583 55948.* Large, just outside city walls. Speciality thick, nutritious soups. Large wicker flasks of light red on the tables.
Erasmo
Ponte a Moriano *Tel: 0583 406362* Beside the Colline Lucchesi with large garden. Traditional *trattoria* with tasty food. House, local or Tuscan wine.
I Diavoletti
Camigliano *Tel: 0583 929547*

COLLINE LUCCHESI

Lucca's low hills rise like butterfly wings either side of the River Serchio that flows south towards the town. It is a comparatively rainy zone, the damp westerly air from the sea rising as it meets the hills and being pushed into black clouds. In theory the Sangivoese reds are Chianti-like but softer and fruitier, the whites, produced from Trebbiano and others, are light, fresh and crisp. Sadly, however, most producers are more enthusiastic about their art than their winemaking skill, disappointing wines abound.

The western wing can be seen within half an hour. Leave Lucca on the road to Abetone, almost immediately turning left towards Camaiore across the River Serchio. Within five minutes you arrive at Cappella. On the right are the neatly ranked vineyards of the Le Murelle. Turn back on yourself and then right at the third bridge over the Freddana Stream – a matter of seconds – to Mutigliano. Just before the church on the right, turn left and amble down to Monte San Quirico and back to Lucca.

A *trattoria*, pizzeria, bar and meeting point. Choose fish, vegetarian or Lucca-style menus. Full range of Italian wines.
La Nina
Montecarlo *Tel: 0583 22178*
Grilled meats the speciality. Broad Tuscan wine list. Pricey.

ENOTECHE

Petroni Lucca, Via Beccheria 30
Keen selection of Lucca and Italian (and French) wines. Also oil, honey.
Mindi Montecarlo, località Turchetto
Wines from all over the world plus oil, honey, jams and preserves.

FOOD SHOPPING

Lucca Market Piazza Anfiteatro
Wednesday and Saturday.
Pasticceria Pinelli
Lucca, Via Beccheria 28.
Traditional desserts and cakes.
L'Antica Bottega del Prospero
Lucca, Via Santa Lucia 13. Preserves plus cereals, pulses, herbs etc.
Bar-Pasticceria Alessandro Paolinelli Piaggione 11km north of Lucca, but worth the journey for typical chestnut-flour sweetmeats.

AGRITURISMO

Most wine estates have *agriturismi* including: **Fattoria Maionchi** (see above) **Fattoria di Fubbiano** *Tel: 0583 978011/978311* **Fattoria Colleverde** *Tel: 0583 402262* **Villa Lenzi** *Tel: 0583 295187*

The best views of the eastern hills can be seen when leaving Lucca northward towards Abetone. Branch right onto a tiny road to Pescia. Within a couple of minutes you see the church of San Pancrazio across to your left and the vineyards of La Badiola. Most of the views are to the right, however, as the road cuts through at high level, looking down on an amphitheatre of vines and olives. Just past Matraia is a lay-by on the right from where to survey the whole scene. The pink buildings down to the right belong to Fattoria Colleverde, which uses a Piemontese consultant. After about ten minutes of slow driving take the right turn to Camigliano. Make sure you see the superlative Villa Torrigiani before turning left again to Tofori. You pass Fattoria Maionchi on the right, from where signs lead to Fattoria di Fubbiano. You can then turn back to Lucca or proceed eastward into the zone of Bianco della Valdinievole (see p130).

Lucca to Florence

BIANCO DELLA VALDINIEVOLE

The Nievole River valley runs along the eastern edge of this area, not through its heartland around Cozzile. Vineyards appear in occasional clumps, well separated, although there is quite a lot of abandoned terracing. The wine, mainly from Trebbiano, is light, crisp and sometimes a little fizzy; most is drunk locally. There is also a Vin Santo. The area of production, however, is diverse, visually wonderful, quite different from other parts of Tuscany and well deserving of the couple of hours it takes to see it properly.

If you are coming straight from Lucca, head for Pescia, joining the route at the Collodi turn-off. Otherwise, leave the Colline Lucchesi, through the glorious, olive-drenched scenery of Petrognano and San Gennaro. From there take the road downward (if in doubt, turn left), overlooking the reservoirs of the plain below, eventually following a sign to Collodi across the valley.

Next make for Pescia where there is a choice. If you feel brave, cross the river, then fork left and head towards Malocchio. This route quickly becomes a narrow, rutted track but is a pretty short-cut to Cozzile. For scenic bliss and the more general view, do not cross the river but continue northwards towards Vellano. After a little lowish land (similar to Chianti Rufina) along the narrow river valley, the road zig-zags up through dense pine forests blanketing the precipitous slopes. From the northernmost extreme there are fine views over the lower land. You may also see the 2,000m peak of Mount Cimone, about 25 kilometres away.

Wind down the road back into olive grove scenery, punctuated by occasional vines, to Cozzile, Massa (another one) and the outskirts of Montecatini. There branch left, ascending to Vico, then to Serravalle Pistoiese, before swinging back along and under the motorway to

BIANCO VALDINIEVOLE

RECOMMENDED PRODUCER

Fattoria di Montellori
Fucechio
Tel: 0571 242625
The estate has numerous plots of land: some practically flat, some excellently exposed, some close to the estate, some as far away as Cerreto Guidi and Montalbano. Continual innovations have helped to realise the potential of Empoli's hills. A wide range of characterful wines.

RESTAURANTS

Cecco
Pescia *Tel: 0572 477955*
Sound restaurant; good, traditional dishes. Fagioli, asparagus (in season), veal-stuffed ravioli, *la fiorentina*, ice-cream with hot berry fruits sauce. Simple wine list.

Monte a Pescia
Tel: 0572 476887
The name both of the restaurant and the place. A wide range of meats cooked over an open fire, typical Tuscan dishes.

La Romantica
Massa e Cozzile
Tel: 0572 601000
Classic Tuscan dishes cooked with verve. Small but thoughtfully assembled wine list. No credit cards.

La Cantina
Monsummano Terme
Tel: 0572 53173
Spacious, comfortable *trattoria* decorated with wine barrels of all sizes. Flavour-rich, traditional dishes. Game stew is the focal point. Drink house wine or choose a bottle from shelves on the walls.

Cucina di Giovanni, Enoteca Giovanni
Montecatini Terme
Tel: 0572 71695
Confusingly, 'Enoteca' is the restaurant, 'Cucina' the *trattoria*. Go to the *trattoria* for the simplest traditional food with a good bottle of wine; or to the restaurant for Tuscan inventiveness. Extensive cellar.

La Panzanella
Empoli *Tel: 0571 78347*
Easy-going, friendly *trattoria*, known especially for its first courses. Carefully selected wine list. All inexpensive and good value.

Right *The stunning façade of the Palazzo Vescovile in San Miniato, on the edge of the Colline Pisane.*

Above *An ancient church in the wonderful castellated village of San Miniato.*
Left *Old-fashioned wicker-encased bottles of Bianco dell'Empolese.*

Monsummano. This leads through the southern spur of the area which has completely different countryside: open, flat-tish, and intensively cultivated.

BIANCO DELL'EMPOLESE

Between Puntone and Stabbia the road crosses into the pretty Bianco dell'Empolese area. Empoli's wines are made chiefly from Trebbiano with some Vin Santo too. The zone is more extensive than Valdinievole but the vineyards of any merit are concentrated around Fucecchio to the south. So continue along the same road for ten to 15 minutes to see increasing numbers of vines draped graciously across the hills until, approaching Fucecchio, they surround you completely.

From Fucecchio you can cross the river Arno to see the castellated jewel of San Miniato on the edge of the Colline Pisane, or go straight to Empoli, a large commercial town. Heading along the river, the low slopes of Empoli's hills form a backdrop to the left and within minutes, once you reach Colle Alberti, the wine zone also extends to your right. With its neat fields and square-towered villas the scene starts to look more like central Tuscany, and a sense of well-being hangs in the air.

SPAS

Montecatini Terme
The town oozes wealth, vigour and glitz. There are smart bars, restaurants and hotels, bustle and bright lights. The spa itself is huge and supremely elegant, with marble avenues fronting the treatment areas and much ceremony surrounding the dispensing of its waters.

Monsummano Terme
Wide range of treatments but for full benefit go underground in the Grotta Giusti where the hot springs emerge through a submerged lake.

FOOD SHOPPING

Pasticceria Bargilli, Pasticceria Desideri
Viale Grocco 2 and Via Gorizia 5, Montecatini Terme. The places to go for Montecatini's own sweetmeat, *cialde*, sliced almonds and sugar encased in a pair of wafers.

PLACES OF INTEREST

Truffle fair and market
November
San Miniato is an important centre for white truffle hunting. To find out more, contact the Associazione Tartufai delle Colline Samminiatesi. *Tel: 0571 42014.*

Collodi
The mother of Pinocchio's author (Carlo Lorenzini) was born in Collodi, and in her honour used Collodi as a pen name. The commemorative Parco di Pinocchio has superb gardens punctuated by various sculptures of the long-nosed anti-hero.

Carmignano

Carmignano is a small zone bounded by the Prato plain and the high Monte Albano which gives its name to the surrounding Chianti Montalbano zone. Carmignano lies in Monte Albano's rain shadow and benefits from cool air from its slopes, giving better growing conditions than further west.

The wine, now DOCG, is from one of the first demarcated zones – defined in 1716. It was also the first DOC to permit Cabernet Sauvignon in its Chianti-esque blend, due to Count Ugo Contini Bonacossi of the Capezzana estate. He argued that Cabernet was probably brought to the area from France by the Medicis in the 18th century and was as 'traditional' a grape as any in the area. DOC committees eventually agreed to allow Cabernet in the blend.

Carmignano is distinguished by its elegance and finesse. The best, marked by an almost perfect balance, live for decades

Right *The tiny village of Carmignano has some delightful old features such as this alcoved wall.*

CARMIGNANO

RECOMMENDED PRODUCERS

Tenuta di Capezzana
Tel: 055 8706091
Run by the amiable, hospitable Count Ugo Contini Bonacossi and family, this large estate has a range of supremely fine wines, olive oil and grappa.

Artimino
Tel: 055 8792051
Huge estate with wines that have improved dramatically recently. Concentrates on reds wines Carmignano, Carmignano Riserva Medicea, Barco Reale, Chianti Montalbano and Comigoli, a young, light, Chianti-style wine. Also Vin Santo.

Il Poggiolo
Tel: 055 8711242
Slow-maturing wines, beginning to get noticed. Carmignano, Barco Reale, Vinruspo, Vin Santo, and olive oil.

Fattoria Ambra
Tel: 055 8719049
Working hard to improve wine quality. Produces mainly Carmignano, including cru versions Le Vigne Alte and Vigna Santa Cristina a Pilli.

CHIANTI COLLI FIORENTINI

RECOMMENDED PRODUCERS

The western Chianti Colli Fiorentini vineyards stretch over the hills south of the Arno to San Gimignano and eastwards to Chianti Classico.

Fattoria Le Calvana
Montagnana Val di Pesa
Tel: 0371 671073

Fattoria Sonino
Montespertoli *Tel: 0571 609198*

Lanciola
Galluzzo (in Florence's southern suburbs). *Tel: 055 208324*

HOTELS

Artimino
Tel: 055 8718081
High-class hotel on Artimino estate.

Hotel Hermitage
Poggio a Caiano. *Tel: 055 212208*
Comfortable, modern hotel. Spacious rooms, swimming pool.

although are drinkable almost from day one. A lighter style is also made, named Barco Reale di Carmignano after a long Medici boundary wall which still stands. There is also a rosé 'Vinruspo', Vin Santo and red Vin Santo Occhio di Pernice.

Carmignano can be reached easily from Empoli or Florence. In either case make for Lastra a Signa or Signa to reach Ponte a Signa, which crosses the Arno. From Lastra cross to north of the river, then turn left, following a slim road along its north bank. After a few minutes, follow a sign to the right to Artimino. This marks the beginning of the zone. Wind upwards past well tended vines to walled Artimino. The villa, once a Medici hunting lodge, and its adjacent hotel and restaurant complex are just outside the tiny village. From there, amble through peaceful, vine-clad scenery to La Serra and on to Carmignano itself, near the vineyards of Il Poggiolo. Next head for Santa Cristina (direction Vinci) and see wonderful views back eastwards over Florence. You may even be able to pick out the Duomo.

Past Santa Cristina the road begins to rise onto the pine-clad slopes of Monte Albano. Just as you think you are leaving the zone well behind, there is a road to the right (not on most maps) that takes you to Bacchereto. It skirts under the mountain for a couple of kilometres and brings you onto the second side of Carmignano's saddle-like formation. From

RESTAURANTS

Da Delfina
Carmignano, località Artimino
Tel: 055 8718074. Elegant, well-appointed place, attentive to detail. Menu based on local, seasonal ingredients: good use of vegetables throughout the traditionally-based meal. Carefully selected wine list. Not cheap but worth the price.

Ovidio
Agliana *Tel: 0574 718065.* Friendly *trattoria* serving traditional fare based on seasonal availability. Good wine list. Ovidio himself is adept at matching wine to your chosen meal.

La Limonaia
Pistoia *Tel: 0573 400453*
In Gello, 2km from the town centre. Once used for lemon storage. Dishes based on the traditional with modern touches. Wines from all Tuscany.

Oavaldo Baroncelli
Prato *Tel: 0574 23810.* Smart, small. Choice of traditional and inventive dishes. Well chosen, well priced wines. Quite costly but good value.

Barni
Prato *Tel: 0574 20635.* Wine bar behind delicatessen (see below). Small choice of well-cooked Tuscan food.

Logli
Prato, frazione Filettole. *Tel: 0574 23010.* 2km from the centre in olive-clad hills with fine views. Long-standing, popular restaurant, large, rustic and typical with a huge, mainly Tuscan wine-list and filling, tasty food.

Above left *The large villa just outside the tiny village of Artimino (left) was used by the Medicis as a hunting lodge. There is now a hotel/restaurant complex alongside.* Top *Grandeur mixes with rustic in Artimino.*

FOOD SHOPPING

Caffé Valiani
Pistoia
Good coffee, tarts and amazing situation. Actually part of the baptistery of San Giovanni Fuoricivitas church and still has frescoes on the walls and a terrific ceiling.

Panetteria Gastronomica Capecchi
Via Dalmazia 445, Pistoia
Not just bread but the typical local sweetmeats (including *cantucci*), and prepared delicatessen-type dishes.

Biscottificio Antonio Mattei
Via Ricasoli 20-22, Prato
The place to go for *biscotti di Prato* and maybe a cake to take home.

Barni
Via Ferucci 24, Prato
Delicatessen with enormous choice. Wine bar behind.

L'Arte del Cioccolato
Via Provinciale 378, Agliana
Aptly named. Don't miss chocolates filled with Vin Santo – fabulous.

Main picture *Pistoia's striking striped Cathedral of San Zeno.* Below and far right *Relaxing in the bars and restaurants of Pistoia.* Bottom *The colourful old hospital frieze, one of several treasures in this elegant town.*

Bacchereto there is a sign to Capezzana, the area's top estate. Skirt past the villa of Bacchereto (detour left to see the estate), then follow the road through the hillside. Florence appears in front of you. Just when you think the city is so close you must have come too far you pass a tiny chapel, then the cellars (both right), and estate buildings (left) of Capezzana. Twist down the narrow, cypress-lined avenue back to reality and the rather mundane village of Seano.

You could now pass through Poggio a Caiano, where Fattoria Ambra is based, to return to Florence, or take the motorway. But first it is well worth taking a look at the well-heeled towns of Pistoia and Prato.

PISTOIA

Just 20 minutes from Seano, Pistoia is an elegant place with smart shops and a quiet hum of people going about their business. Of Roman origins and later important as a banking centre, it suffered from its position

ENOTECA

L'Enoteca
Via Provinciale, Agliana. Great selection from all Italy and abroad.

PLACES OF INTEREST

Poggio a Caiano
Superb Palladian-style 15th-century Medici villa with gardens overlooking the village. Now used as a museum.

Agliana
Home of the coffee production house of Trinci (brand Tricaffé).

SPECIAL EVENTS

Giostra dell'Orso Pistoia
July: ceremonial jousting between 12 knights and a (wooden) bear.

Display of the Virgin's Holy Girdle
Doubting Thomas believed the Assumption of Mary only when, in heaven, she removed her girdle and gave it to him. This relic apparently stayed intact until crusaders brought it back to Prato Cathedral in the 12th century. It is exhibited five times a year.

between continually warring Florence and Lucca. Its solid city walls and gates contain the Piazza del Duomo, with its green and white striped Cathedral of San Zeno, bell tower and baptistery. Pistoians feel their elegant town has at least as much to offer as Florence. Indeed it is more attractive in that there are far fewer tourists crowding the narrow streets and souvenir-stalls littering the stylish displays of Italian chic.

PRATO

Approached through a dreary mass of industrial sprawl. (The road via Montale is the least dull and gives you the opportunity of seeing a final estate, Tenuta di Bagnolo at Montemurlo, Tel: 0574 652439.) Prato has the industrious feel of a bustling northern city – it has been famous for textiles since the 12th century, and they are still important there. Almost as famous are the *biscotti di Prato*, long, crunchy almond biscuits like *cantucci* that are often dunked in Vin Santo. The solid city walls of the medieval centre and the rugged 13th-century Norman-style castle (the only one in Tuscany) reflect the town's hard-working atmosphere.

Now go safely back to Florence – and start all over again.

GLOSSARY

Alberese – limestone soil, renowned for vineyards in Chianti Classico

Acquavite – spirit, distilled from grapes or other fruit

Affinamento – keeping newly-bottled wine before release, to soften it a little

Alimentari – small, general food store

Aurelia (Via) – the first main state road, the SS1, built by Mussolini. Follows the coast from Rome to the French border. Successive constructions now give a choice of a 'new' or an 'old' Aurelia as well as a motorway in places. Often referred to in speech and on road signs

Autostrada – motorway, tolls are payable

Azienda – estate

Azienda agricola, azienda agraria – estate making wine from own grapes

Azienda vinicola – estate making wine from bought-in grapes

Azienda vitivinicola – estate making wine from both own and bought-in grapes

Barrique – small oak wine cask, most commonly of 225 litres, sometimes 500, made from French oak and used either new or up to the third year of age. Not traditional but increasingly common.

Botte (*pl* botti) – traditional wine cask, usually of Slavonian oak, large (25hl plus) and kept for many years

Bruschetta (*pl* bruschette) – toasted Tuscan bread, rubbed with garlic and drenched in olive oil; may also come with tomatoes, black cabbage or other topping

Cacioteria – unusual, local terminology for cheese shop

Campanile – bell tower

Cantina Sociale (*pl* cantine sociali) – cooperative winemaking and/or bottling cellar

Cantucci/cantuccini – hard, crispy biscuits with almond slivers, best dunked into Vin Santo

Caratelli – small casks, typically about 50 litres, used for maturing Vin Santo

Casa colonica (*pl* case coloniche) – traditional farmworker's house

Cassia (Via) – the second main state road, the SS2, leading from Rome, through Siena to Florence (see also Aurelia)

Chiantigiana – the road that cuts right through Chianti Classico

Classico – the central, classic heart-land of any wine zone; usually classico wines are better than non-classico (called normale)

Colli (*sing* colle) – hills

Colline (*sing* collina) – small hills

Comune – commune or parish; smallest self-governing geographical unit

Consorzio (*pl* consorzi) – a voluntary body set up to protect its members' interests; controls standards, and assists with marketing strategies.

Cru – unofficial but frequently used term for wine from single vineyard

Enoteca (*pl* enoteche) – wine shop; often used also to mean winebar or wine shop with tastings Enoiteca – official word for wine shop with tastings, infrequently used

Fagioli – white kidney beans

Farro – a barley-like grain, used in soups and first courses

Fattoria – farm or estate (factory is **fabbrica**)

Fiaschetteria – old fashioned Florentine term for wine shop

Frantoio – olive oil crushing and pressing plant

Frazione – literally fraction; part of a commune or parish with its own name and identity

Frizzante –lightly sparkling

Fiume – river

Galestro – clay-schist soil important for quality in Chianti Classico

Gastronomia – delicatessen, also sells prepared dishes

Governo – traditional practice, once almost abandoned, now staging a comeback, in making Chianti; some grapes are held back, then added to the just-fermented wine later to restart the fermentation; benefits/drawbacks disputed

Grappa – spirit made from grape lees (qv)

Hectare (Ha) – measurement of area, about 2.47 acres

Hectolitre (Hl) – 100 litres

La Fiorentina – a large, T-bone steak, usually for two people and a great speciality

Lees – mass of skins and stalks left after a wine's fermentation

Località – small locality, similar to Frazione (qv)

Macelleria – butcher

Maceration – seeping of grape skins in the grape juice

Mercatino – flea market

Mercato – market

Mezzadria – old crop-sharing system

Must – grape juice

Normale – non-Riserva wine (qv)

Panetteria – bread shop

Passeggiata – common Tuscan (and Italian) practice of going for a stroll in the early evening; more than a leg-stretch it's an important people-watching, mating and gossip-gathering occasion; each town has own, never-changing times and routes

Passito – wine made from dried or semi-dried grapes

Pasticceria – pastry shop

Pecorino – ewe's milk cheese

Pizzicheria – local Florentine term for *gastronomia* (qv)

Podere (*pl* poderi) – small farm or plot

Provincia – province, administrative unit between regione and commune (qv)

Quintale (*pl* quintali) – unit of weight, equal to 100 kilos

Regione – region, largest Italian administrative unit; there are 20 of which Tuscany is one

Resa – yield of volume of grape must expressed as a percentage of grape weight, most commonly 70%

Ribollita – a soup based on vegetables cooked at length, thickened with bread

Riserva – wine, usually from a better year or a particular selection of grapes, aged longer than normal. Minimum length of ageing is controlled by wine law and differs from wine to wine.

Salumeria – shop selling salumi (see below)

Salumi – cured meats: salami, prosciutto etc, and occasionally fish (salt cod, anchovies and the like)

Sformato – a type of vegetable mousse, often served as a main course accompaniment

S.P. – strada provinciale, provincial road; each province has own numbering system

S.S. – strada statale, state road; one system of numbering throughout Italy

Sulphur dioxide (SO2) – an antioxidant of necessity used in all wine; undetectable and harmless if quantities carefully restricted

Superstrada – fast, toll-free, dual carriageway road

Torrente – small stream, often no more than a trickle but subject to occasional surges

Varietà – grape variety

Varietal – a grape variety

Vin Santo – a (usually) sweet wine made from grapes left to dry for about three months after the harvest

Vintage – harvest; the year the wine was made

GAZETTEER

INDEX

Indexer's note: Towns are given in brackets for hotels and restaurants

PICTURE CREDITS

Front cover **Robert Harding Picture Library/Walter Rawlings**
Back cover **Reed International Books Ltd/Michael Boys**

Jason Lowe 9 top, 12 bottom left, 13 bottom right, 44, 53, 68 top, 73 bottom, 76 bottom, 98/99, 100 bottom, 101 top, 102, 103, 104/105, 106 centre, 106 bottom, 108, 109, 110/111, 111 top, 112 bottom, 113 bottom, 115, 116/117 top, 117 top right, 120, 121, 122/123 top, 122 bottom left, 123 bottom, 125 top left, 125 top right, 127 bottom right, 128 bottom, 128 top left, 129 bottom, 131, 132, 133 centre, 134/135 top, 134 bottom left, 134 centre left .
Reed International Books Ltd/Michael Boys 43, 74, 75 top, 76/77 top, 93 top, /**Alan Williams** 2, 14/15 bottom, 22/23, 25 top, 27, 29 bottom, 34, 36/37 top, 39, 45 top right, 45 top left, 48/49 bottom, 56 bottom, 57 bottom, 65 centre, 70, 83, 94 top, 95 top, 96, 106/107 top, 114, 117 bottom right, 133 top.
John Ferro Sims 3, 5, 7, 8/9, 10, 12/13 top, 12/13 bottom, 14 top, 15 top, 16, 17, 18/19, 20, 21, 24/25, 26, 28, 29 top, 30/31, 32/33, 35, 36 bottom, 38, 40/41, 45 bottom right, 46 bottom left, 46/47, 48 top left, 49 top, 50/51, 52, 54/55 top, 55 bottom right, 56/57 top, 58, 59, 60/61, 62/63, 64, 65 top, 65 bottom, 66, 67, 68/69, 71, 72, 73 top, 75 bottom, 78, 79, 80/81, 84, 86/87, 88, 89, 90/91, 92 top, 92 bottom left, 92/93 bottom, 93 bottom right, 94 bottom, 95 bottom, 97, 100 top, 101 bottom, 107, 110 bottom left, 111 centre right, 112 top, 113 top, 118, 119, 122 centre left, 123 top right, 124, 125 bottom, 126 left, 126/127 bottom, 127 top right, 128/129 top, 130, 133 bottom, 135 top right.

ACKNOWLEDGEMENTS

Other people's acknowledgements are hardly ever of great interest and from time to time I've wondered why authors didn't just thank the people personally and leave it at that. But I didn't realise how much the help of people along the way matters when writing a book, how they can make the seemingly impossible happen and, vitally, how they can keep your morale topped up. It was also a source of amazement and pleasure that so many people were willingly prepared to offer so much time and expertise, often at very short notice, even those for whom the project can bring no benefit at all. It would be unthinkable not to acknowledge such magnificent assistance publicly and permanently. So I abundantly thank:

Ursula Thurner, Consorzio del Marchio Storico, who started me off, set the tone, made me realise the scope and that it was attainable, who was assiduous in the preparation and execution of her days with me and opened my eyes to so much;
Bruno & Elyane Moos, whose weekend I ruined, whom I totally exhausted but who still kept smiling - and came back for more. They made an ace Directory Enquiries service too. I don't know what I'd have done without them;
Christine, who give new meaning to the sound of a cockerel, who deserves a very long list of thank yous but instead will be rewarded by a return trip to Livorno for drawing the short straw;
Liz, who sacrificed the tastings she was hoping for to cover all the wine-free bits and who made all the hard work fun;
Giuseppe Mazzocolin, who was continually interrupted by innumerable faxes from me but answered them anyway, whom I managed not to see three times in succession, who was plagued by misfortune in getting me certain documentation but who was still invaluable;
Francesco Giuntini, who will be terribly disgruntled that he's not mentioned first in this list but will at least be relieved to know he's in front of
Ugo Contini who never batted an eyelid when I turned up at incredibly short notice and who succinctly filled me in on Carmignano in his usual efficient, charming manner.
Faith Heller-Willinger whose support and advice at the end of a phone line gave eating in Tuscany a new perspective.
Franca Spinola, President, Camera di Commerzio IAA di Grosseto;
Roberto Saletti, Camera di Commerzio IAA Grosseto;
Giacomo Regina, Camera di Commerzio IAA Grosseto;
Valter Nunziatini, Amm Reg Provincia di Grosseto,
Giovanni Prisco, AIS;
Paolo Solini, Consorzio Vino Nobile di Montepulciano, who covered an amazing amount of ground in exhaustive detail,
Stefano Campatelli, Consorzio Brunello di Montalcino, as ever diligent, detailed and enthusiastic and with the rare skill of making a tough, unenviable task seem a pleasure.
Marie-Sylvie Haniez-Melosi, Movimento Nazionale del Turismo di Vino, who not only provided some incredibly useful pointers but, with her husband Roberto, gave me one of the most fun evenings I've had in Italy in a long time;
Paolo Valdastri, literary life-saver of Livorno;
Angelica Faguioli, who set me straight on San Gimignano;
Maria Pia Maionchi, for relaxed hospitality and comprehensive information on Lucca;
My parents, they'll know why;
Plus all the Gamberi and Arcigolosi who, unknowingly, pointed me in the right directions for good eating places and food and all the other people who, knowingly or not, got me through.
Above all, a big thank you to Stephanie for the editorial support I'd so often heard about but never before experienced and to Sue for stepping magnificently into the breach.

Erratum: Maureen Ashley lectures and holds tutored tastings on Italian wines for the Italian Trade Centre.